Ethics
in
Modern
Management

ETHICS
IN
MODERN
MANAGEMENT

GERALD J. WILLIAMS

QUORUM BOOKS
New York • Westport, Connecticut • London

Library of Congress Cataloging-in-Publication Data

Williams, Gerald J.
    Ethics in modern management / Gerald J. Williams.
      p. cm.
    Includes bibliographical references and index.
    ISBN 0–89930–707–8 (alk. paper)
    1. Business ethics. 2. Industrial management—Moral and ethical
aspects. I. Title.
    HF5387.W53   1992
    174′.4—dc20   91–44991

British Library Cataloguing in Publication Data is available.

Library of Congress Catalog Card Number: 91–44991
ISBN: 0–89930–707–8

First published in 1992

Quorum Books, One Madison Avenue, New York, NY 10010
An imprint of Greenwood Publishing Group, Inc.

Printed in the United States of America

The paper used in this book complies with the
Permanent Paper Standard issued by the National
Information Standards Organization (Z39.48–1984).

10 9 8 7 6 5 4 3 2 1

To Ann, Stephen, Helen, Mary Ann, John, Kathleen,
my Mother and Father, and the Oblates of Mary Immaculate.
A.M.D.G.

Contents

Preface

I have written this book with the people in mind who have to make moral decisions every day in the marketplace. I have selected the world of business as its focus simply because I spent nearly 33 years there, and I believe I have some understanding of the moral conflicts and the anguish that often goes along with trying to resolve them. My experience has led me to believe that business managers need a solid base for reflective thinking on and a serious commitment to a set of conscientiously-held moral principles to help them make sound moral decisions.

What is true about moral reflection and decision making for business people is true, of course, for all human beings in whatever circumstances or occupations they find themselves. Consequently, people in the "non-business" world may find this book useful, especially if they are managers in organizations that are not devoted to profits but to human services, for example, nursing and medical practice in hospitals, community-service groups, or even government. Professors in business schools, and their students may also find the book helpful.

The book is an attempt at applied ethics. Two moral theories, utilitarianism and the Thomistic version of natural law, are examined and their principles applied to specific cases. The cases are also considered in the light of cultural moral relativism. This process, of course, leaves considerable room for error in judgment. The conclusions I arrive at in discussing the cases are surely open to challenge. That may be precisely what will make the book interesting: if it stimulates thought and discussion, even if only critical of my thinking, it will have served its purpose.

Acknowledgments

I want to acknowledge the assistance I have received from many people. Adelaide Thomason, O.S.U. of the College of New Rochelle has provided me with an opportunity to teach business ethics for the past seven years. Russell Taylor, Chair of the Business Department at the College of New Rochelle, was a prime mover in getting the business ethics course started and has supported it by working it into the business curriculum and encouraging his business students to take it. I am indebted as well to my students, whose insights and questions have been helpful in clarifying issues and looking at them from new perspectives. James Hollowell and Maurice McCarthy, two of the most ethical business people I know, along with several people from Seton Hall University—William Smith, David O'Connor, and Alexander Butrym—provided many helpful comments and suggestions. I am especially grateful to my daughter, Helen Williams, for her invaluable editorial assistance.

I also want to thank The New York Times Company, the editors of *The Progressive*, and the editors of *The National Catholic Reporter* for the use of material from their publications.

Finally, my sincere thanks to Eric Valentine, my publisher, for his most helpful comments, suggestions, and support.

1

Introduction

IS THERE AN ETHICAL CRISIS IN THE AMERICAN BUSINESS COMMUNITY?

A few years ago, Amitai Etzioni (1985), University Professor at the George Washington University, made an analysis of court and other public documents involving the Fortune 500 companies. He determined that:

> Between 1975 and 1984, 62 percent of the 500 corporations were involved in one or more illegal incidents; 42 percent, in two or more; 15 percent, in five or more. The episodes included, among others, price-fixing and overcharging, domestic and foreign bribes, fraud and deception (for example, falsification of tax records to conceal political contributions and deceptive bookkeeping) and patent infringements.[1]

In the 1980s, the news media were full of stories about alleged or actual unethical business behavior.[2] Currently, newspapers, journals, and TV news programs have carried numerous accounts of the savings and loan debacle that has produced some of the worst cases of business fraud, at least in terms of its financial impact on the taxpayers, in U.S. history. Other prominent stories have featured, for example, Salomon's involvement in the treasury securities scandal, allegations that Wall Street

firms and banks inflated orders in their bidding for the Federal Home
Loan Mortgage Corporation's securities and submitted false information
to that Agency, and the Bank of Credit and Commerce International's
guilty pleas to several criminal charges.

Is the proliferation of these stories about business wrongdoing simply
a result of media "hype"? Or has there been a decline of crisis proportions
in the morality of American business people? That may be too strong
a claim, but it is clear that the general public doesn't have a high
regard for business's reputation. According to a New York Times poll
taken in 1985, "only 32 percent of the public thinks most corporate
executives are honest, while 55 percent think most are not."[3] I don't
believe that opinion has gotten any better, and I think it's a mistake
to rely on public relations gimmicks to restore the good reputation of
business in general. Only business people themselves can do that by
raising their ethical consciousness as it relates to their operations, by
reflecting on possible reasons why incidents of fraud, cheating, lying,
and theft, generally considered to be immoral on their face, appear to
be more and more commonplace in the business community. Business
people need to think about ways to stop or at least significantly reduce
immoral business practices.

To initiate this reflective process, let's consider a few examples
illustrating the kinds of business situations that raise moral questions.
Here are several cases reported by *The New York Times*:

- The Securities and Exchange Commission accused the Paradyne Corporation of using fraudulent tactics to win a $100 million computer contract
  from the Social Security Administration. Because Paradyne's own
  computers were not ready at the time of its scheduled presentation, the
  S.E.C. charged, the company showed the Social Security Administration
  another company's computer with Paradyne's name on it.[4]

The Company later pleaded guilty to conspiring to defraud The Social
Security Administration (G. DeGeorge, 1987).

- Ametek Inc., a military contractor, . . . agreed to pay $5.2 million in
  civil and criminal fines to settle accusations that it had overbilled the
  Government for sonar systems used on Navy Submarines.[5]
- (A) Navy official, Stuart E. Berlin, admitted in United States District
  Court in Alexandria, Va., that he had made false statements, committed
  wire fraud and received a bribe in exchange for providing consultants

with inside information that helped two companies bid for military contracts.[6]

Two other famous cases widely reported:

Based on a cost-benefit analysis which included estimating the monetary value of a human life, the Ford Motor Company allegedly decided not to modify the design of the gas tank in its early Pinto car and truck models even though the company's own tests showed a high likelihood that the tank would catch fire in the event of rear-end collisions occurring at certain speeds.

Lockheed Corporation made payments to government officials and other people in foreign countries to insure winning contracts to sell its jumbo jets.

All of these examples involve actions that at first blush seem to be morally suspect as apparent instances of deceit, bribery, and disregard for consumer safety. If that is true, and if the people involved in the incidents were guilty, why were they willing to act the way they did? Perhaps they did not see anything morally wrong in what they were doing, even though some of the actions in the cases were judged to be illegal. Reflecting on these cases raises the further question: Why do any business people act in ways that seem to be or are in fact immoral?

Some years ago, W. Michael Blumenthal, a chief executive officer of the Bendix Corporation who served as Secretary of the Treasury in the Carter Administration, thought that the increase in business misbehavior was simply due to the changes occurring in society's moral standards. As he saw it, "Changes have also taken place in the standards of moral behavior that now apply to business. Activities once considered as normal practices are now unacceptable."[7] People, then, may just be caught in the changing tide of moral standards, and what they thought was morally correct in the past suddenly is not seen that way now. They don't see themselves any less moral just because society's expectations have changed.

Robert Jackall, Professor of Sociology and Chairman of the Department of Anthropology and Sociology at Williams College, may have come closer to the real answer. He conducted extensive interviews with managers at all levels in several American corporations asking them about the moral dilemmas they faced in their everyday business-life circumstances. In his published findings, Jackall reports one executive's response which may well represent the kind of moral thinking too many American managers use in their business lives. According to this executive, what is right in the corporation is not what's right in a man's home or his church. "What is right in the corporation is what the guy above you wants from you. That's what morality is in the corporation." (Jackall, 1988).

In effect, a good many business people seem to suffer from a moral schizophrenia which drives them to perform actions in the business world that they might never attempt to justify in their private, personal-life circumstances. How to account for this apparent moral malady?

Pure self-interest or just plain greed may be the simplest explanation: people may be willing to do whatever they have to do to insure the success of their corporations or businesses because that is where they find their identities, their reputations in the community, their ticket to financial well-being for themselves and their families. On the other hand, nonselfish motives may also be at work; perhaps many managers truly believe that the vitality and well-being of their communities or the country depend in very large measure on the success of their economic enterprises. They may believe that whatever is good for business is good for the political and social structures in which those businesses operate, and that, as a consequence, the business world *has* to have a moral system which differs, necessarily, from the set of moral principles that govern nonbusiness-life situations.

It is also possible, of course, that managers do not apply their personal moral principles in their business lives simply because they are afraid of losing their colleagues' esteem, their opportunities for advancement, or even their jobs. Regrettably and understandably, they may be victims of their own moral weakness, a failure we find not just among business managers, but in our political, government, educational, and health-care communities as well.

THE PURPOSE OF THIS BOOK

This book is intended to help the business executives and managers who read it give conscientious thought to the moral rationales they use in their own day-to-day business situations and decide whether or not they lead to sound ethical conclusions. The first step in the process is to examine briefly and better understand how a moral theory produces the principles and beliefs people use to justify their behavior ethically. The next step is to reflect on, in the context of moral theory, the obligations business people have to communities, employees, customers, and stockholders. Part of the method for carrying on this reflection will be to make a moral analysis of cases, hypothetical and actual, and attempt to apply to the actions (not the actors) involved the principles of the moral theories that will be described in the next chapters. Then, I argue that we have to begin to repair the moral reputation of business by eliminating the idea of a "double ethic," the notion that the moral principles governing our private lives simply cannot always be applied in our business lives. Finally, I suggest some steps individual managers might take to improve the moral climate of their workplace and some steps corporate officers should take to insure that high standards of ethical conduct permeate their organizations.

SUMMARY

It appears that a good many Americans, in the context of their business lives, are acting in ways that are contrary to ordinary morality. The reasons for these actions probably vary all the way from simple greed and inordinate self-interest to believing that what they're doing isn't immoral at all because the well-being of their local, state, and national communities depends on how well their business enterprises are doing. They may conclude, therefore, that separate moralities are needed for business and private circumstances. This book is intended to help managers think through the moral rationales they use in business settings and decide whether they lead them to sound ethical decisions. It examines both real-life and hypothetical kinds of situations in the light of selected moral theories and offers reasons why there cannot be separate moralities for business and private lives. It also suggests steps that individuals and corporate leaders might take to improve the moral climate of their businesses.

I begin by examining, in the next chapter, moral theories that provide grounds for deciding whether an action is morally right or wrong. First I look at what a moral theory is then at a shortened description of selected moral theories. Readers who may be interested in an expanded treatment of these theories will find it in the Appendix where they are described in much greater detail.

NOTES

1. Etzioni, Amitai. "Shady Corporate Practices," *The New York Times*, November 15, 1985, p. A35. Copyright © 1985 by The New York Times Company. Reprinted by permission.

2. Just three "for instances": (1) *New York Magazine* published a study, "What Price Ethics" in its July 14, 1986 issue, on morality in the eighties. (2)

The May 25, 1987 issue of *Time*, focusing on the moral disarray in American political, religious, government, and business institutions included accounts of some notable cases of alleged and actual business misconduct. (3) Nearly every headline on the front page of *The New York Times* for August 5, 1988 was devoted to some type of actual or alleged business fraud.

3. Clymer, Adam. "Low marks for Executive Honesty," *The New York Times*, June 9, 1985, Section 3, p. 1. Copyright © 1985 by The New York Times Company. Reprinted by permission.

4. Pollack, Andrew. "Issue of Deceit in Electronics," *The New York Times*, March 31, 1983, p. D2. Copyright © 1983 by The New York Times Company. Reprinted by permission.

5. Lev, Michael. "Guilty Plea on Billing by Ametek," *The New York Times*, July 31, 1990, p. D4. Copyright © 1990 by The New York Times Company. Reprinted by permission.

6. Wines, Michael. "Two Plead Guilty to a Conspiracy in Pentagon Case," *The New York Times*, March 24, 1989, p. A1. Copyright © 1989 by The New York Times Company. Reprinted by permission.

7. Blumenthal, W. Michael. "Business Morality Has Not Deteriorated—Society Has Changed," *The New York Times*, January 9, 1977, sec. 4, p. 9. Copyright © 1977 by The New York Times Company. Reprinted by permission.

2

Moral Theories

MORAL DECISION MAKING IN THE BUSINESS WORLD

John Dewey and James Tufts (1932) pointed out the conflict a person runs into when

> (he) goes from a protected home life into the stress of competitive business, and finds that moral standards which apply in one do not hold in the other. . . . If he tries to face (the conflict) in thought, he will search for a reasonable principle by which to decide where the right really lies. In so doing, he enters into the domain of moral theory.

For many business people, good (correct) moral decisions may often seem to fly in the face of good business decisions, and they need to figure out how to address this apparent incongruity. They can't do so, as I see it, without first having some understanding of how moral principles are derived and how they may be applied in the context of everyday business activities. In subsequent chapters of this book, we'll be doing just that, applying principles derived from utilitarian and natural-law moral theory to business situations involving moral conflicts. We'll also be looking at how cultural moral relativism sees them.

Let's do a sort of preview of just how this process works. As we'll see in more detail, utilitarianism holds that we should always produce the most good consequences on the whole, the greatest good for the greatest number, if we want to act rightly. Natural-law theory argues that we must look to our human nature to determine what's best for us, that our human reason, reflecting on that nature, will tell us how to act. Natural-law moralists claim that certain actions like murder, suicide, and theft are always wrong and may never be done under any circumstances. Cultural relativism claims that society's laws, mores, or customs alone tell us what is right or wrong. To get a better feel for all of this, imagine yourself as the principal actor in the following cases:

Case 1

You are a senior analyst in a corporation that evaluates companies for possible mergers and acquisitions. If you juggled the figures on a certain company's financial statement, it would look like a good candidate for a takeover. Your firm would receive a hefty fee from the acquiring company and your own outlook for increased salary and advancement would improve significantly.

Here are some of the key good and bad consequences to be weighed:

- Your company's profits will be enhanced allowing it to pay higher salaries to employees and higher dividends to shareholders.
- Your own financial and career interests will be enhanced.
- The acquiring company may find itself with a company that is not financially viable and may incur severe losses as a result.
- Your company's reputation and long-term prospects would be harmed if your deception became known. Your own personal reputation and future would be jeopardized as well.

The utilitarian would likely believe that the bad consequences would outweigh the good ones in this case, and would say that changing the figures would be morally wrong.

The natural-law moralist would see this as a clear-cut case of deception, lying, an action that is morally wrong in itself and, therefore, forbidden.

The cultural relativist would ask whether this act was against society's laws or customs. If so, it would be wrong to do it.

Case 2

Your construction firm is in the process of building a shopping center in a large city. The city's building inspectors make it clear that unless they receive a few thousand dollars in cash payments under the table, there will be significant delays in approving your work. These delays would cost you tens of thousands of dollars.

The good consequences resulting from making the payments:

- Your company would avoid financial loss.
- Your client would get the job on schedule. Your reputation for getting your work done on time would be preserved.

Some bad consequences:

- You would be contributing to the moral corruption of the inspectors who are entrusted with making objective assessments of your work.
- If your payments were found out, you would be subject to fines. Your firm's reputation would suffer.
- Your firm's profits would be reduced unless you knew about the need for making these payments before starting construction and included them in your bid. In that case, the cost of the project to your client would be unfairly inflated.

If there was no likelihood that blowing the whistle on these inspectors would put them out of business and it was unlikely that you would be found out, the utilitarian moralist might agree that it would be acceptable to make the payments, given an overall weighing of the good and bad consequences.

The natural-law moralist would likely see making the payments as cooperating in another's evil action and contributing to the corruption of officials who have a duty to the people they serve. These officials are not entitled to ask for these payments, and are committing a dishonest act by extorting them from contractors. The right thing to do would be to report the requests to the proper city authorities. If experience showed, however, that the authorities continually looked the other way at this practice and would ignore your report, the natural-law moralist might consider you a victim of extortion who was coerced into making the payments.

The cultural relativist would want to know, before deciding whether making these payments was moral or not, whether society expected them to be made as a matter of doing business, as, perhaps, an acceptable way to make up for the low salaries these inspectors might be getting, or whether they violated the law or social customs.

Case 3

You're the purchasing manager of a large corporation that needs to buy a sophisticated, expensive computer system to manage its operations efficiently. A supplier offers you two percent of the sales price if you will give his company the contract for the system. His system is a quality one, well within the range of the specifications set in the request for bids. It will cost more than the others (because it probably includes your two-percent payment) but not so much that it would appear to be way out of line. Of course, your company has a code of ethics that forbids accepting payments or gratuities of any kind from suppliers. You signed that code.

The good consequences if you agree to the supplier's proposition:

- You enhance your own financial situation.
- The supplier and his company's shareholders do well on the contract.
- The system functions as your company wants it to.

The bad consequences:

- You will lose your job (and, quite possibly, your reputation and future prospects for a well-paying job, perhaps) if your company finds out about the payment.
- Your company's reputation might be tarnished, at least for a short time, if your action became public knowledge.
- Your company might have to pay more than it should for the system. If so, fewer resources are available for higher salaries and dividends or for reinvestment in the business.
- The other bidding companies lose financially because of the money they expended on submitting a bid that won't be considered on its merits. If one of them should have been selected instead of the one who paid you off, its employees and shareholders lose out on any prospects for higher salaries or dividends.

I believe that the utilitarian would suggest that the bad consequences in this case outweigh the good ones, and it would be morally wrong to accept the payment.

The natural-law moralist would argue that if you accepted the payment, you would be violating your fiduciary responsibility to the company to get the best system at the least cost. That's what you are paid for and what you agreed to do when you took the position. You would be perpetrating an injustice to your company. In addition, you would be treating all the other suppliers who had submitted their bids in good faith unjustly.

The cultural relativist would ask whether this kind of behavior was commonly accepted in the society in which it occurred. If it was against the customary practices in the society or against the law, it would not be morally acceptable to engage in it.

Case 4

Your company makes pacemakers for people with heart problems. It is aware that there is a good probability that the pacemaker may suddenly fail and endanger the wearer's life. Should that fact be concealed in the advertising and other promotional material for your product?

The consequences of concealing it:

- The company's finances are protected—especially if a majority of its profits are riding on this product. Employees and shareholders will benefit from the money to be made on it.

The bad consequences:

- A heart patient using the pacemaker might have his or her life endangered if it should suddenly fail.
- The company's reputation would suffer if its failure to disclose this possibility became known; it would also be subject to penalties under the Food and Drug laws and would suffer financially.

In this case, the utilitarian would probably see the danger to a human being's life as outweighing the impact on the company if it didn't conceal this defeat. The *probability* of failure, to the extent it could be known, would have to play a big part in this judgment.

The natural-law moralist would likely see this as a form of deception since people would probably not buy the pacemaker if they knew about this flaw. The deception would be wrong in itself and forbidden, regardless of the consequences to the company.

Since concealing the pacemaker's defect would most likely violate the law, the cultural relativist would probably see it as an immoral act.

Case 5

You run an advertising agency. A client company that will pay you a hefty fee wants your company to design a series of ads that make unsubstantiated, misleading claims about its product.

The good consequences of going along with the client:

- Your company and its shareholders make a lot of money.
- The client company and its shareholders make a lot of money from the sales your ads produce.

The bad consequences:

- The customers lose money because they don't get what they paid for. If the product is a health-care item, for instance, that won't deliver what it's said to, it might even harm them.
- Your company's and your client's reputations (and your respective shareholders) will suffer if the deception is found out. Civil penalties may be involved.

The utilitarian moralist would see this kind of advertising as morally questionable, considering all the consequences involved.

The natural-law moralist would regard such claims as lies, as inherently morally wrong on that account alone. The wrong would be further compounded if there was a threat to human health or life.

The cultural relativist would ask whether any law or custom was being violated. If so, it would be morally wrong to produce these ads.

Case 6

Your company deals in investments. You ask another firm to sell the shares of one of your client companies ("dump" them, in effect) in order to drive down their price, because you are going to market these shares later for your client in a special offering. The lower price will allow you to sell this offering more easily. That will mean more commissions for your firm. You tell the company that is going to dump these shares that your company will make up any losses it incurs.

Some good consequences:

- Your company and its shareholders will make more money.

- The firm you asked to sell the shares will not incur any losses.
- Buyers will be able to obtain your client's shares at a lower price.

The bad consequences:

- Your client will probably not realize as much value from its offering as it would if the share prices were higher.
- Your company's reputation will suffer if your action is found out. Civil and even criminal penalties may be involved. Your shareholders will probably suffer financial losses.
- The company that agrees to dump the shares may, if its action is found out, be subject to civil and criminal penalties. Its employees and shareholders would suffer financial losses as a result.

The utilitarian moralist will likely argue that this action is immoral, after weighing and comparing all the consequences.

The natural-law moralist will see a failure here to carry out a fiduciary responsibility to serve a client's interests—as an investment company ordinarily contracts to do. The company would, in effect, be breaking a promise to its client to look out for its interest. There is an element of deception clearly present here in manipulating the buying and selling of shares; that is morally wrong in itself.

The cultural relativist would determine whether there was a law against this kind of activity and would consider violating it immoral. If no law existed, then whatever was "customary" would be acceptable.

WHAT MORAL THEORIES ARE ALL ABOUT

Our family upbringing, formal and informal education, and socialization combine to provide us with a set of moral principles and beliefs that help us resolve ethical dilemmas. Moral theorists provide an underlying rationale for establishing and judging such principles and beliefs.

Some moralists, called relativists, claim that there is no universal standard of right conduct and would never consider any action morally wrong in itself. According to some of these moralists, the customs and rules of each social group are the criteria for judging what is morally right or wrong for members of that group. They argue, for example, that adultery is wrong only if a particular society's customs or laws say it is. Other relativists claim that morality reduces merely to emotion, to feelings of approval or disapproval of an action. In any case, moral relativists argue that there is no way to derive a universal moral standard from reason.

Theorists called moral absolutists argue that there is one universal standard for judging what is right and maintain that reason can show us what that is. For some of them, certain actions are always morally wrong in themselves, independently of circumstances or social customs and conditions. Murder, for instance, the direct and deliberate killing of an innocent person, is always wrong and may never be committed—no matter how many good consequences would result from doing it.

In the long history of ethics, philosophers and theologians have generated a number of moral theories. For our limited purposes here, I will describe just two of them, utilitarianism and the Thomistic version of natural law, that base their principles on a moral standard but differ about what the standard is and what specific obligations it generates. These two theories also illustrate the common distinction between *teleological* moral theories, which derive moral obligation solely from an action's consequences and *deontological* theories, which derive moral obligation from grounds other than consequences.

I will also outline cultural moral relativism, a theory about morality that holds there is no objective moral standard at all, that morality depends solely on the practices, customs, or mores of a particular society.

CULTURAL MORAL RELATIVISM

One approach to moral decision making is to claim that there is no one moral standard after all, no objective measure of right or wrong, that all morality is relative to the customs, mores, practices, or laws of a particular culture or society. To decide, for example, whether bribery is right or wrong, we only need to ask what the relevant society or culture where the question of bribery arises thinks about it.

Every society, past and present, is characterized by a moral code of some kind. According to cultural anthropologists and sociologists, these codes have differed and do differ among societies. Practices one society or culture has approved of have been forbidden by others: for example, killing unwanted babies, burning witches, polygamy, incest, torture, inhumane methods of imprisonment. Moral codes, then, are not developed from some external standard, they are not the product of reason, and they vary from culture to culture.

This theory about morality makes moral decision making simple. To know what to do or refrain from doing in any given situation, a person just follows the customs, mores, or laws of the culture or society he or she happens to be in at the time. It could be especially appealing to business people who might think it easier to operate in a society where bribery and kick-backs to government officials seem to be the way of life, or where there are no laws against pollution, or laws requiring safe conditions in the workplace, labeling products that might be dangerous to people's health, or paying a minimum wage. Of course, the other side of the coin is that local customs and laws may be so restrictive that they might make doing business in a particular community impractical or even impossible.

This view of morality is powerfully persuasive to many people, but it does run into some serious theoretical difficulties. One of the arguments that may be used to establish its validity is that because there are a great variety of human moral codes, a standard of morality that could guide all human beings everywhere at all times in all situations cannot possibly exist. This reasoning is logically fallacious, however, because it moves from what "is," the *fact* of variety in moral practices to the broad conclusion that a universal moral standard is impossible. But simple differences in moral behavior do not, by themselves, guarantee a true conclusion about the existence or nonexistence of a moral standard. Further, there do seem to be common values among all societies. Murder, if accepted, would threaten the very existence of a society, and no culture seems to find it acceptable. Life in society would be chaos unless people refrained from stealing the property of others and kept their promises to each other. Every society seems to have sexual mores whose underlying thrust is to protect the community, however they may differ from other communities' sexual practices. So differences in mores, if closely examined, may rest on common, universal, foundations.

Another theoretical difficulty for cultural moral relativism is that in the absence of a universal moral standard acceptable to everyone, there is no way of ever judging that certain moral practices are better than others, that one society is more moral than others. A society that approved polygamy, infanticide, slavery and genocide, for instance, could be judged no worse, morally speaking, than one that prohibited these practices. People in a given society could never justify making it better by way of deep philosophical reflection and moral argument.

There is also the problem of deciding just what a particular culture is, just what group of people a society includes. It may be a simple matter to define a group in primitive conditions where it's evident that a particular set of people are a separate "tribe" with their own customs and traditions, but it is obviously more difficult in complex societies. In the United States, for instance, certain subgroups may believe that polygamy or homosexuality is morally acceptable, or may adopt religious practices or experiences like snake-handling or smoking peyote. People in the larger community, however, may find these customs objectionable. How does one determine which group's customs or mores should be followed?

Or, take the difference between the *laws* established by a community and its *customs*. Which has preference, morally speaking? The law may prohibit speeding over 55 m.p.h. but the majority of the people in the community may customarily ignore it and average 65 m.p.h. Adultery may be illegal but that law may never be enforced because the custom in the community may be for everyone to mind his or her own business. There may be laws against bribing government officials but it may be that "everybody does it." In effect, do the laws or its "customary" practices define the mores of the community? Which prevail as the moral rules to be followed?

Finally, where *does* the obligation to obey the mores or laws of a society come from? Why do its members observe them? Are they simply afraid of punishment or social ostracism? If so, do people only obey when there's a chance of being caught in a violation? Or do they obey from some deep feeling of duty to their ancestral traditions or their culture's way of life? If they obey because their obedience contributes to the common good, they are sneaking in a standard to be measured against, and, strictly speaking, they are no longer relativists.

In the analysis of moral problems in subsequent chapters, I assume that the cultural moral relativist acknowledges an obligation to obey whatever mores or laws a society's members embrace.

Let's consider now two moral theories that do argue for one universal standard of morality.

UTILITARIANISM

The moral theory known as "utilitarianism" holds that

- An action is to be judged morally right in a given situation if it produces the most "happiness," expressed as "good consequences," overall, "on the whole," or, as is often stated, the "greatest good for the greatest number." Each person's good counts for one and only one.
- A moral agent has to calculate the good and bad consequences his or her action will produce, and determine which will predominate when

the action is performed: whether the good will outweigh the bad, or vice-versa.

- No action (for example, directly and deliberately killing an innocent person) is ever morally good or bad in itself; that judgment has to wait until its net good or bad consequences have been calculated. If the good consequences outweigh the bad, the action is morally right; if the other way around, it is morally wrong. This calculus alone determines the action's morality. Some moralists consider utilitarianism a relativist theory, one that "yields different results under different conditions" (Abelson & Friquenon, 1987), although others consider it absolutist in the sense that it appeals ultimately to one universal standard of right action—the most good on the whole (Hospers, 1972).

- The intention with which the act is performed is not, by itself, morally significant.

Some moralists object to the theory because it may allow the end to justify the means: an action that will produce overall good consequences must sometimes be done, however heinous it may seem in itself. It might, for example, be necessary to kill some innocent people directly in order to save a greater number of lives. Or it might be necessary to punish innocent people in order to deter others from committing certain crimes. The theory does not seem to leave room for justice to override consequences in certain situations.

THOMISTIC NATURAL LAW

The species of natural law moral theory described here was developed principally by St. Thomas Aquinas; that's why it's called "Thomistic." Its essential characteristics include

- Human reason reflects on the kind of being we are, our inclinations, our physiological, psychological, and rational make-up, and determines what is in our best interests, our well-being. Our ultimate goal is "happiness."

- Once it has determined what is good for us, reason commands (legislates) actions that promote our well-being and forbids those that don't.

- In legislating what actions we must do and avoid, reason reflects the "eternal law," what God, the creator of our human nature, has in mind for beings like us, how we are to act.

For the natural-law theorist, certain actions are intrinsically wrong because they are always contrary to human well-being: murder, suicide, theft, lying, rape. They may never be committed, no matter how many good consequences might result from them, and this obligation extends to all people everywhere at all times in virtue of their common human nature. That's why this theory is absolutist.

It's not enough, in this theory, to just do a good action; our intention must always be to do good. A good act performed with an evil intention becomes morally wrong, it condones evil and vitiates our character. Additionally, circumstances affect an act that otherwise is good in itself: sexual relations, for example, are good in themselves, but not when done with someone who is not your spouse.

One apparent drawback of the theory is that it forbids some actions even though significant good consequences might result from them. Directly killing one innocent person, for instance, is never allowed, even if it would save many lives. Natural-law theorists do recognize, however, that an action that causes both good and evil effects may sometimes be legitimate. They follow, in these cases, the double effect principle that has these provisions:

- an action that produces both good and evil effects has to be good or at least morally indifferent in itself before it may be done;
- the agent may intend only the good effect; the evil effect is seen as a regrettable, unintended side effect of the action that necessarily accompanies it;
- the evil effect may never be the *means by which* the good effect is achieved; otherwise the agent would be directly intending evil;
- there has to be a due proportion between the good and evil effects; the evil may not outweigh the good.

If any of these provisions is violated, the action is morally wrong.

DIFFERENT MORAL THEORIES MAY YIELD DIFFERENT MORAL PRINCIPLES

It should be evident from the consideration of just these two moral theories and cultural moral relativism that different principles for guiding ethical decision making may be derived from different grounds of moral obligation. Because of this, it is important for people who want to feel comfortable, ethically speaking, with their business decisions (or any moral decision) to reflect conscientiously on the theoretical basis for the set of moral principles and beliefs they hold. They need to decide whether they are satisfied that it is sound or whether they need to adopt another set derived from a more convincing moral theory.

SUMMARY

To better understand and resolve moral conflicts we encounter in our business lives, we need to reflect, in the light of moral theory, on the moral beliefs we hold.

A moral theory provides reasons, grounds for determining whether an action is morally right or wrong. According to some theories, there is one universal moral standard for everyone (moral absolutism) or there is no such standard (moral relativism). Some moralists hold that there are certain actions wrong in themselves, for example, murder, suicide, lying, and no reason ever justifies performing them. Others believe that no action can be judged immoral in itself; circumstances and social conditions will play the decisive role in determining whether or not a given action is wrong.

Cultural moral relativism argues that moral obligation lies solely in the customs or mores or laws of a culture or society. To be moral, one must obey society's accepted practices. But cultural moral relativism has its own weaknesses. Its proponents commit a logical fallacy when they argue from the fact of different cultural practices to the conclusion that no universal moral standard is possible. It doesn't provide a way to judge one society better than another or to argue from deep philosophical reflection that a particular society could be made morally "better." It may also fail to recognize that there may really be a universal moral foundation disguised by cultural differences. Finally, it's not always easy to determine where a particular culture or society begins and ends, where one clear set of practices are accepted by a given population.

We saw that utilitarianism looks to overall consequences on the whole as the sole criterion for deciding whether an action is right. Although this theory may have a strong attraction for practical-minded business people, it has some shortcomings. It seems that producing overall good consequences in certain circumstances might infringe on the rights of individuals or override considerations of justice. The end might justify the means, however heinous they may seem.

Thomistic natural-law theory looks to human nature, its intellectual, physical, and psychological characteristics as the measure of morality. An action that promotes the human person's well-being is morally right; one that detracts from it is morally wrong. For Aquinas, reason, reflecting on human nature, promulgates the dos and don'ts of the natural law and, in so doing, reflects what the eternal law of God who created human nature wants for that nature. Consequences are useful in deciding whether a particular action is morally right or wrong. But they are not the ultimate criterion for that judgment.

One problem this theory poses for some people is that it regards certain actions as intrinsically wrong (for example, murder, suicide, and lying) and never allows them—even if they would produce significant good consequences overall. This difficulty is offset somewhat by the theory's use of the double-effect principle under which a person may directly produce a good effect even though it is necessarily accompanied by an evil effect. This is morally acceptable as long as the act the agent does is morally good in itself or at least morally indifferent. The agent must not intend the evil effect or use it as the means to achieve the good effect. Finally, there must be a due proportion between the two effects.

An examination of these approaches to morality clearly shows that different theories generate different principles for judging actions morally right or wrong. That's why business people need to reflect on their own principles and determine whether they are comfortable with them or whether they need to convert to some other theory's principles.

3

Human Dignity and Justice

In the previous chapter, we looked at the grounds of moral obligation offered by utilitarianism, Thomistic natural law, and cultural relativism. Before leaving the topic of moral theory, two fundamental moral concepts bear some separate elaboration: the dignity of the human person and justice. Both concepts have a significant bearing, for many moralists, on the resolution of moral problems. This is true for the natural-law moralists we talked about earlier. For the utilitarian, human dignity and justice are morally important only to the extent that they fit into the calculus of good and bad consequences a particular action or rule of action may produce. The cultural relativist would not likely appeal to these concepts explicitly to resolve a moral issue, but they may well be part of the inexplicitly expressed foundation of the practices, customs, or mores of any culture.

HUMAN DIGNITY

That every human being has intrinsic worth is rooted, for religious believers, in the idea that God has created each of us in His own image and likeness. For others, the worth of human beings is a fundamental intuition which all reasonable persons simply accept. The philosopher

Immanuel Kant (1724–1804), for example, thought along these lines holding as a categorical imperative, one evident to human reason and binding absolutely, that we must treat everyone as an end and never only as a means.

It follows, for many moralists, that in virtue of this human dignity, just as human beings, people have certain rights not given to them by any other person or by any human authority. The rights to life, to learn, to use the world's material resources, to be free from attacks on our person by others, to marry and found a family are conspicuous examples. The only justification for interfering with these rights arises in situations where other human rights might have some more morally compelling claim.

In this account, one of our most basic moral obligations is respect for the human person.

JUSTICE

The definition of "business" that concerns us, of course, is the exchange of goods and services that occur "in the marketplace," among buyers and sellers of material commodities or personal services of some kind. The primary moral principle or virtue ordinarily thought to govern these transactions is justice. Whole treatises have been written on what justice is, but for our purposes we'll use a simple definition: "to render each person his or her due." The specific variety of justice that is of primary concern here is commonly called "commutative" because it governs transactions and agreements (contracts) between equals, that is, individual persons or groups that may be treated as if they were individual persons.

Distributive justice, another species of justice, governs the relations between any community (the state, primarily) and its members. It requires that each member of the community get his or her fair share of the benefits that are to be "distributed" in the community. Distributive justice applies in the business world where issues, for example, of affirmative action, equal employment opportunity, plant closings, and use of natural resources are concerned.

A prime consideration in analyzing business ethics problems, then, will be determining what justice requires of the people involved in these problems, what rights, or claims, are set up to provide or receive goods or services when equal parties in the community contract in the marketplace. It's important as well to consider what business enterprises owe the members of the community beyond just supplying these goods and services.

SUMMARY

For many moralists, the dignity, of the human person and justice are two concepts that are of prime importance in resolving moral problems. Human dignity is the source of fundamental human rights that belong to people simply in virtue of their humanity, and these rights may not be set aside except for valid claims based on the rights of others. We have a serious moral obligation, then, to show respect for human persons.

Justice requires that we render each person his or her due. Commutative justice has to do with the business transactions occurring between individuals or groups that are treated as persons. Distributive justice governs the obligations arising between a community and its members, the distribution of benefits associated with being a member of that community. Our concern, of course, will be with what distributive justice may require of business managers.

4

Moral Responsibility

CONDITIONS FOR MORAL ACCOUNTABILITY AND LIABILITY

Once we're satisfied that we are comfortable with the grounds for deciding whether an action is morally right or wrong, we need to know when to hold a person morally accountable for his or her actions. Legal liability is not the issue here. A business executive or manager involved in a case of ethical misconduct may or may not be found legally guilty of a crime but in itself, that has no bearing on the person's moral responsibility for what was done. A finding of not guilty may only mean that the prosecution didn't present a convincing case to a jury and that the accused party didn't incur any kind of legal liability. A person's *moral* responsibility, however, may still remain, and he or she may still have to make restitution for money stolen, or property damaged or destroyed, or for physical or psychological harm done to others. Company officials or managers charged with but not convicted of illegally dumping toxic waste, for example, may still have a moral obligation to make restitution for any harm they have done to people or their property. So it's important to understand and reflect on the conditions for judging a person's moral accountability for his or her conduct.

KNOWLEDGE AND FREEDOM

To be morally responsible for an action, a person must act intentionally and deliberately, that is, must be fully aware of what he or she is doing and must act freely, without any physical or psychological coercion. To the extent that a person's knowledge or freedom is diminished or absent, moral accountability and liability are proportionately diminished or even nonexistent. (The same principle is used in the legal system where degrees of responsibility are recognized: homicide, for example, ranges from cold-blooded murder to involuntary manslaughter.)

IGNORANCE

Ignorance excuses an agent only when it is nonculpable, when the person acting does not understand the nature of what is being done or cannot anticipate all the reasonably foreseeable consequences of an action. The question of ignorance is sometimes subtle in business situations. Suppose, for instance, that managers in a particular division of a company were submitting padded expense vouchers to recover personal contributions made to political candidates, payments that would be illegal if made directly by the company. Now, the top executive in a division is ordinarily considered responsible for his or her subordinates' actions, but in this case, there would probably be several layers of supervision between him or her and these managers, and he or she would not be expected to know about the inflated expense accounts unless and until they were uncovered in an audit or reported some other way. But if that executive had hinted somewhere along the line that he or she didn't expect people to make these contributions out of their own pockets and didn't want to know how they were going to get their money back, he or she would surely be culpably ignorant of their actions and would consequently share in the moral (if not legal) responsibility for what they did.

COERCION

It's probably easier to determine whether ignorance excuses a person in a particular situation than it is to judge to what degree coercion diminishes moral responsibility. A bank teller who hands over the contents of a cash drawer to an armed robber is clearly not morally guilty of misappropriating the bank's assets. But what about situations where business people have to cooperate in some apparent moral evil initiated by others? I have in mind cases where higher levels of management in a company may ask or order a subordinate or a contractor to carry out an action that may harm other people or their property or is simply dishonest: for example, dumping toxic waste where it will pollute a community's water supply; figuring out ways to fire or demote a whistle blower or other employee who is an aggravation to management in some way; ignoring hazardous safety conditions which would be very expensive to correct; altering financial reports to hide evidence of mismanagement or downright dishonesty; concealing a supervisor's personal or profligate spending in padded expense vouchers; hiding political contributions in fake expense accounts; or acquiescing in a customer's morally questionable demands just to avoid losing a valuable client. How much coercion is involved in these examples? Is an employee's moral accountability lessened just because the boss or higher management (including, perhaps, a company officer) or a customer told him or her to do any of these things? May an employee claim that it is the boss or the company or the customer who is really acting, and that he or she is just following orders? Consider two hypothetical cases.

(1) Suppose that a large American firm wants to establish a potentially highly profitable account with a foreign company whose officials are biased against female business executives and make it clear that they do not want to deal with them. The firm's top managers deliberately exclude their women executives from any of the business or social meetings with these officials, thereby abetting their immoral (and, in the United States, probably illegal) discriminatory behavior. Could the firm's management claim coercion on the grounds that it would very likely lose this account if it were to ignore its customer's cultural sensibilities?

(2) Suppose that an individual employed by a company that manufactures nuclear weapons decides that what his company is doing is morally wrong. It is probably unlikely that the company will shut down its operations because of his moral scruples, but is he obliged to stop cooperating in what he considers a moral evil and resign? What if he couldn't make as much money in some other job, money needed to complete his children's college educations or pay off some burdensome debt? What if his pension eligibility is only two years away and he can't transfer it to some other industry? Is the threat to his financial security strong enough to justify his staying on the job for a few more years?

Consider this case about claims on a state-sponsored insurance fund:

an adjuster used by several (auto insurance) companies to examine reported losses of electronic equipment, said he became increasingly nervous about being asked to approve claims without seeing the vehicles. He said he was asked to verify that tape decks and car phones had been stolen, but realized after his inspections that the vehicles had never had the reported equipment. When he balked at some of the more flagrant requests, Mr. Altman said, he began to lose business, and when his whistle-blowing became known he was blackballed.[1]

Could an adjuster in this kind of situation claim coercion if he went ahead with the approvals and subsequently argued that the insurance companies, not he, were morally responsible for the fraudulent claims?

THE NATURAL-LAW SOLUTION TO THE CASES

Let's see how a Thomistic natural-law moralist would likely resolve these cases, and then contrast that approach with the utilitarian's.

The natural-law moralist holds that to the extent an action is involuntary, the person performing it is proportionately less responsible for it. Now, both violence and fear may make an action involuntary. If I am tortured beyond my endurance and forced to do something evil, I can't be held responsible for my action because of the physical violence done to me. In the three cases just described, however, physical violence is not the issue; grave fear of losing one's livelihood or profits is. Is this fear enough to make the cooperation of the people involved in these cases involuntary, coerced? It depends on whether their cooperation is considered formal or material.

Formal cooperation means that an agent becomes a willing partner with another person in performing an intrinsically wrong act, consenting to and approving the evil done. Formal cooperation is never justified, even by grave fear. (I personally believe that in some cases, fear can be so severe that it amounts to violence.) Material cooperation, by contrast, means that a person is asked to do something that is morally legitimate in itself, not evil by its nature, but ultimately helps another person accomplish an act that is intrinsically wrong. In this case, the person who is asked to perform the morally good or indifferent act may do so for a good reason, intending its good effects while simply tolerating the evil effects stemming from what the other person does. Grave fear can make material cooperation morally legitimate in some circumstances.

The Discrimination Case

Let's try to apply these principles starting with the first hypothetical case where a firm's executives are being asked to exclude women from participation in an activity which is purely and simply part of ordinary business dealings. It's hard to see why this action is not morally wrong in itself since the act of discriminating against someone on the basis of a characteristic (gender) which is irrelevant to job performance is a serious affront to the dignity and worth of a human being. On the natural law account, I believe, the firm's executives would be guilty of formal cooperation in their customer's evil action if they excluded women from participating in a business activity, and the fear of losing the customer's account would not excuse them.

The Nuclear Plant Case

Now, let's look at the second hypothetical case where an individual has come to believe that the production of nuclear or chemical weapons is immoral in itself. How do we judge whether his cooperation is formal or material? For the sake of argument, let's assume that the continued production of these weapons is in fact immoral because they are a dire threat to millions of human beings if they are ever used in a global war and because the government for which they are being made fully intends to use them if it has to.

First, we need to ask what this person's job in this company is. Are his talent and knowledge vital to making these weapons? Is he a nuclear scientist whose expertise is nearly irreplaceable or can only be replaced at considerable cost and grave inconvenience to the company? If so, it would seem that his work is so immediately tied to the final product that what he does has to be considered formal cooperation in a moral evil, and fear of losing his job or pension would not justify his staying on with the company. If he is performing some less sophisticated function not absolutely vital to the process, his fear of losing his livelihood or his pension might justify his staying on until he can retire or until he finds a job that will pay as well as this one.

The Insurance Case

In the third case, an insurance adjuster claims that he is being asked to lie, to commit a direct act of fraud which is morally wrong in itself. If he inflates the estimates, he is cooperating formally in the evil intended by the insurance companies, and the fear of being blackballed or losing some accounts would not justify his action.

THE UTILITARIAN SOLUTION TO THE CASES

The utilitarian moralist has to decide what to do in each of these kinds of cases by determining what action will produce the most net good consequences overall, keeping in mind that the agent's advantage doesn't count any more than the advantage of everyone else involved in the situation. Any threat to an individual's well-being has to be added in as just one more of the overall consequences to be considered, and coercion, by itself, doesn't override the requirement to weigh all consequences equitably.

The Discrimination Case

Let's begin again with the case of the executives who have to decide whether or not to exclude their female employees from any social or business contact with a potential client.

From the utilitarian's standpoint, a decision by top management to come down solely on the side of profit might be criticized as a failure to include all reasonably foreseeable consequences in its calculations; management might be accused of looking out only for its own good instead of the "good on the whole," the good of everyone who could be affected by its action. How would these executives have to proceed, then, as good utilitarians?

To calculate the negative effects of excluding women from these business contacts, top management would have to ask a number of questions. Would the affront to these women cause them serious psychological damage? If they couldn't be persuaded that in the spirit of team play they ought to suffer this indignity for the overall good of the firm on which their own careers depended in the long run, would a significant drop in their morale and trust in the company cause them to perform poorly in their jobs—to their own and the firm's detriment? What would it cost to recruit and train replacements for those women who might resign because they were discriminated against? What would happen if this action became public? Would the company's reputation be damaged to such an extent that it might lose existing and future customers as well as future investors? Would it be able to continue to attract high-quality employees? What would potential lawsuits claiming discrimination cost? What would the effect be on social justice generally, on the effort to promote equal opportunity in the marketplace? Given the difficulty of predicting this last consequence, should it even be a consideration?

On the plus side of the calculation, the company's executives would have to determine whether the increased profits obtained from this new customer's business would allow them to pay higher salaries to themselves and other employees, hire more people, attract new investors who would generate even more profits, pay higher dividends to the firm's owners, and contribute substantially more to the community's overall economic and social welfare. What appear to be purely economic benefits would have to be weighed somehow against less tangible consequences like the effect on the psychological and emotional health of the women executives suffering discrimination.

The process outlined so far looks like nothing more than what would be required for a sound business decision. But it is important to remember that a moral decision is at issue here; we have to determine what the morally right action is. It can be argued that a right moral decision will likely be a good business decision, from a utilitarian viewpoint, but it may well be that what appears to be a good business decision is not necessarily morally right even for a utilitarian who must always determine what is good for everyone, what contributes to happiness "on the whole."

The Nuclear Plant Case

Let's look now at the utilitarian approach to the case of the man employed in the plant making nuclear weapons. His dilemma is whether to continue helping making weapons whose use he believes would be immoral or to quit his job and give up a high salary and other employment benefits that he might not be able to earn in some other occupation.

First of all, this individual has to decide how far to project the consequences of his actions, that is, how immediately or distantly they actually contribute to the production and use of nuclear weapons. Just as it did in the natural law solution, the moral significance of his actions will likely increase the more directly their consequences are tied into the actual production of the weapons. Even at this point, however, the employee might decide that although government officials may in fact intend to use these weapons on civilian populations in a nuclear war, the probability of that happening is sufficiently remote to justify his staying on the job. Remember that the intention of using these weapons against civilian populations is not, by itself, morally significant for the utilitarian as it is for the natural-law moralist who holds that such an intention is in itself immoral. All the utilitarian has to do is decide whether or not the predicted consequences of his or her actions contribute to the good "on the whole."

Finally, remember that any harmful consequences for the engineer and his family have to be given just their own weight along with all other consequences. They don't have any special advantage just because they affect his interests. Coercion by itself is not an excusing condition for the utilitarian.

The Insurance Case

Now let's consider the case of an insurance adjuster who says he was asked to make false claims against a special state-sponsored automobile insurance fund. What consequences should he weigh, "on the whole," in deciding whether or not to go along with the insurance companies pressuring him to make these claims?

First of all, what would happen if he did agree to file them?

- People contributing to the fund might have to pay increased premiums to offset the amounts paid out in false claims.
- If the fraud became public, the adjuster and officials of the companies involved might be prosecuted and fined or sent to jail.
- The adjuster's chances of working for other insurance companies (or anywhere else, for that matter) would be jeopardized because his reputation for honesty would surely suffer. The companies on whose behalf he made the claims would probably lose business because of the damage to their own reputations, and the effect on their profit margins might force them to reduce dividend payments to their stockholders. The adjuster could conclude, however, that if the companies appeared willing to risk this publicity, the likelihood of its occurring must be small, and he wouldn't need to worry about it.
- Finally, it looks like he would have to think about the effect on the insurance industry as a whole if this act of fraud were found out, but that calculation is so complex that he could surely forget it.

On the positive side, filing false claims would save him from economic disaster and would probably increase profits for the companies and their stockholders.

Now, what happens if he refuses to file false claims and reports the companies to the appropriate government agencies?

- If the companies effectively blackballed him, he couldn't continue to earn a living in the insurance business and would have to estimate his chances of working somewhere else at the same salary and level of benefits. The general public would probably admire his honesty, but his reputation as a "whistle blower" would likely work against him in the insurance industry and the work world in general where people who tattle are not popular.

- The adverse publicity that would result from his refusal to cooperate would have a negative effect on the insurance companies who asked him to commit the fraud. They would likely incur legal penalties, would lose customers, and might even be put out of business—bad news, of course, for their employees and stockholders.

- Again, there might be some negative effect on the insurance industry in general, but that would be too tough to calculate as we've already seen.

- He would also have to evaluate the psychological and emotional damage he would personally suffer from the whole episode.

The positive effect of his refusal to commit fraud would be that the people insured by the special fund would not have to pay increased premiums to cover unjustified claims and some unscrupulous companies would be stopped from defrauding present and future customers.

The hard part of the utilitarian judgment in this case, as I see it, is how to accurately balance the losses to all the clients insured by the special fund if the adjuster decided to file fraudulent claims, against his own losses if he refuses to file them. While the financial loss to each individual person insured might be less compared with his, the losses to all of them added together would most likely outweigh his. It certainly is true that his psychological anguish needs to be weighed in the calculation as well, but it is hard to measure that kind of effect against effects that can be expressed in numbers.

Again, coercion by itself doesn't carry any special weight in the utilitarian calculation; it is just one more consideration that has to be weighed with all the others.

THE CULTURAL RELATIVIST'S SOLUTION TO THE CASES

The Discrimination Case

In this situation, we have a conflict of two cultures: the one the firm's officials live in and the one the customer's representatives live in. Whose mores or laws should prevail? To be consistent, it seems to me, a cultural relativist would have to observe the mores or laws of the society in which the business and social events were to take place. Since, in America, excluding the female executives would likely be a violation of U.S. laws against discrimination, and assuming that these laws are the mores of the United States, the executives could not be excluded from any of these business-related functions. I suspect that the company's management could claim diminished responsibility because of coercion only if the law (the mores) recognized coercion as an excuse for not obeying it. Coercion might be a factor in deciding how much to punish someone for breaking a law, if that's a "customary" approach to dealing with lawbreakers in the society.

If the functions were held in the foreign country where the mores (not just the preferences of this particular customer) excluded women from social events or other meetings connected with business, it would be morally correct to keep them away.

The Nuclear Plant Case

In this situation, I believe the cultural relativist would argue that if the nuclear plant was operating under the direction of a legitimate government, that very fact would be sufficient to indicate that society approved the production of nuclear weapons. Therefore, the engineer could continue to work at his job without any moral scruples.

The Insurance Case

As a cultural relativist, the insurance adjuster would have to determine just what mores of his society governed this situation. If the law clearly prohibited making false reports of this kind and he regarded the law as his society's mores, he would have to observe it. If no law were at issue, he would then have to know what his culture expected of people faced with this kind of moral decision. That could only come from his day-in-day-out experience in his society which alone would indicate to him whether everybody believed his or her own interest should always prevail in any situation like this and that nobody would expect him to act against his own interests, that is, under coercion, or whether the prevailing mores would always favor keeping members of the society from harms of this kind. If the latter were true, he would be expected to refuse to file false reports.

SUMMARY

We have now seen how significantly different approaches to morality address the issue of moral liability and accountability for one's actions. They all acknowledge, I believe, as do moralists generally, the principle that people are fully responsible for what they do when they know what they are doing and are not coerced. Moral responsibility is diminished to the extent that knowledge and freedom to act are diminished.

Our key concern was to think about how coercion might get a business person off the moral hook when someone else—the company's management or a customer, for example, wanted him or her to do something morally wrong, or when self-interest was at stake in some morally questionable situation.

We examined three cases where people might have tried to claim coercion as a way of diminishing or eliminating their moral responsibility for their actions: (1) the management of a company trying to win a lucrative account with a potential customer was faced with complying with the customer's cultural preference not to have women present at any business or social meetings. This would mean excluding female executives from activities ordinarily associated with business dealings. (2) An engineer working in a nuclear plant became concerned in conscience that his firm was doing something immoral by building nuclear weapons, and he had to decide whether he could continue to work there or leave and jeopardize his earning power and pension rights. (3) An insurance adjuster claimed to have been asked by auto insurance companies to certify the loss of electronic equipment in cars he had never seen.

We saw that the natural-law moralist justifies the excuse of coercion only in cases where grave fear destroys a person's freedom to consent to an action. These moralists do recognize a distinction between material and formal cooperation in someone else's wrongdoing. Material cooperation means that the action a person performs is morally good or indifferent in itself but someone else uses the action for his or her immoral purposes. Formal cooperation means that a person commits a morally wrong action, intends the moral wrong, and joins his or her action with the morally evil act of another. For the natural-law moralist, material cooperation is sometimes justified for good reasons, usually in a person's self-interest, but formal cooperation in another's evil is never permitted. On this account, a company's executives would formally cooperate in another's evil act of discrimination if they excluded their female executives from business and social meetings. The nuclear engineer would have to decide whether his job, his contribution to producing nuclear warheads, was so essential to the effort that it constituted formal cooperation, and he would have to resign. The insurance adjuster would be committing an act of fraud and his cooperation with the insurance companies would have to be considered formal.

The utilitarian moralist would hold the people involved in the cases accountable for calculating the net good and bad results of their proposed actions and for performing only that action (or acting on a rule) that will produce the most good consequences overall. Coercion by itself does not carry any special weight in the calculation; it is just one consideration among all the others that are at issue.

The cultural relativist locates liability and accountability solely in a society's mores, and coercion is probably an excusing condition only if the society's customary practices acknowledge it as such. In the case of the executives trying to decide whether to exclude women executives from meetings, the mores of the society in which these activities were to take place would have to decide the question. Laws or mores would also have to prevail in the cases of the nuclear plant engineer and the insurance adjuster.

NOTE

1. Sullivan, J. E. "New Jersey Car Insurers Profited on Their Waste," *The New York Times*, August 29, 1989, p. 34. Copyright © 1989 by The New York Times Company. Reprinted by permission.

5

Moral Aspects of Economic Systems

THE MORAL DIMENSIONS OF AN ECONOMIC SYSTEM

Simply put, an economic system is the ongoing process whereby people exchange material goods and personal services in support of the entire range of their human interests. More formally, it is the method a society uses to allocate scarce resources among many possible uses, whether by primitive barter-like transfers or by the highly complex and sophisticated national and international commercial and financial transactions going on in today's economically advanced social and political entities.

How do we specify the moral dimensions of an economic system? By examining what the system must do for people. To start with, we need to reflect on some fundamental truths about material resources and human beings. I will outline here what I believe to be the more significant of these truths without offering extended formal arguments to support them, because I think they are generally plausible, at least in their essential thrust.

First, it is obvious that human physiological, psychological, technological, aesthetic, intellectual, and spiritual needs cannot be satisfied without using natural physical resources. Second, in virtue of the argument offered earlier that every person has worth and dignity, it also follows that everyone has a right to acquire some share of natural resources in order to develop as a human being. While some social and political philosophers argue that every human being has a right to an equal share of natural resources (Dworkin, 1981, 1983), I subscribe to the weaker thesis that every human being has an equal right to acquire and use them. Part of this weaker thesis relies on the notion that because these resources are gratuitously given in nature, no individual has any prima facie claim on or title to any particular set of them, and, consequently, that all resources are there for the use of everyone in proportion to their needs, ability, and the effort they are both able and willing to expend on them. In effect, I reject the idea that justice requires distributing wealth independently of how it is produced, that is, the idea that resources and goods must be distributed equally and that special needs or the effort and talent expended to generate wealth from resources don't count.

I do hold, however, that every individual, including of course, anyone who is physically or mentally unable to personally secure and act on resources, that is, "to work," has a claim on a minimal amount of these resources consistent with what his or her human dignity requires. What that minimum is will certainly change over time, as human knowledge and ingenuity uncover more and more of the potential locked away in nature's raw materials. It seems to me that a minimum share in today's world would at least provide for such basic requirements as an adequate education, decent housing, full participation in political and cultural communities and recreational opportunities, founding and providing for a family, adequate medical care, and provision for old age.

A significant conclusion following from what I have just proposed is that no one may amass and keep a disproportionate amount of resources or the wealth derived from them when other people are unable to obtain the minimum share they need to live at a fully human, decent level.

From these general considerations about natural resources and the economic rights of human beings we can now specify some fundamental moral dimensions of any economic system, dimensions that will help guide the moral judgments made about the business practices which will be treated in subsequent chapters.

First, the key moral virtue that should be operative in the process of exchanging material goods and personal services is justice, rendering each person his or her due.

Second, whatever economic system a particular society has chosen to live under, it must assure everyone participating in it equal access to resources. If there is any practice within the system that blocks an individual or group of individuals from that access, it is unjust. Discrimination in employment, purely on the basis of race, gender, religion, ethnic origin, or handicapped status that denies a person the equal opportunity to acquire and use resources according to his or her needs, talent, and ambition is morally wrong.

Third, no individual or group of individuals may claim a disproportionate share of resources or their products from the economic system. A "disproportionate share" in my mind is measured relative to whether everybody in the system has enough resources to assure that he or she is living at a decent human level.

Finally, the society in which a particular form of economic system is operating has the obligation of securing, through its political structure, access to resources and a fair level of their distribution for all those served by the system. That's why, for example, a society has the moral right to redistribute income through taxation.

While implementing social justice on an international scale is obviously a more complex process than it is in a national community, these basic moral dimensions apply as well to economic activity among nations.

SUMMARY

The moral dimensions of an economic system in which resources are accessed and manipulated and goods and services exchanged and distributed are specified by what it does for people. Everyone has to access physical resources to satisfy their physiological, psychological, technological, aesthetic, intellectual, and spiritual needs, to develop as human beings, and the economic system provides that access.

Resources are given gratuitously in nature; no one has a prima facie title to any of them. Needs, ability, and willingness to expend effort dictate how the products of resources are generated and distributed, so it is not morally required that everyone has the same or equal share of resources or their products. What is required is that all human beings, in virtue of their human dignity, have equal opportunity to access and use them and that each person has a minimum share consistent with that dignity. What a minimum share is will change over time as human ingenuity operates on resources to make them more productive.

A morally sound economic system will insure that justice governs the access to resources and the exchange and distribution of goods and services. It will prohibit any artificial barriers like discrimination on irrelevant grounds that interfere with anyone's access to material needs.

It will insure that no group of people in the system has a disproportionate share of resources; everyone has a right to a "fair" share. The society in which the economic system operates has the obligation to use its government and social agencies to reallocate resources whenever they are unjustly distributed among its members.

6

Employment and Wages

GOOD MANAGEMENT OR GOOD MORALS?

Good managers, as elementary textbooks in business administration readily point out, will attract capable people into the business, keep their turnover low, secure their loyalty to the company and its objectives, and maintain and increase their productivity wherever possible. A business that wants to keep good employees will have to offer competitive salaries along with some kind of health insurance coverage and savings and pension plans as part of its basic wage package—to the extent that its size and financial resources let it. To motivate and satisfy employees, managers also need to provide them with on and off-the-job training; give them effective job-performance feedback; allow them to participate in decisions affecting the structure and objectives of their jobs and how their performance on those jobs will be measured; provide opportunities for them to move to higher-paying positions with more responsibility; tell them whether or not they are promotable; see to it that they have formal and informal avenues of appeal to higher supervision without fear of retaliation from their immediate bosses; and provide them with safe working conditions.

While all of these practices constitute "good management," they have a moral dimension as well. A company's managers may ignore or abuse them ostensibly in the interest of the company's bottom line, but such actions are morally wrong whenever they involve some form of injury or injustice to an individual or a failure to render the respect due someone as a person.

What moral claims, rights, do employees have against their employers as far as employment and wages are concerned?

Let's start, in this chapter, with rights to employment and just wages.

IS THERE A MORAL RIGHT TO EMPLOYMENT?

In the last 10 years or so, many American plants and industries elected to shut down or relocate their operations or downsize their work forces, putting many thousands of people out of work. According to one estimate, "These and similar cutbacks will bring the number of American professional and managerial positions eliminated since 1979 to over 1.5 million."[1]

Some downsizing of American corporations was probably accomplished by ordinary attrition and retirements, but many of the employees affected by these changes had to start over with new employers, perhaps in totally different careers, and some of them likely suffered economic loss along with a severe psychological blow to their self-esteem.

Someone might argue that the people involved in these shutdowns, relocations, and force reductions also suffered a violation of their right to employment, but the argument so stated begs the question of whether such a moral right can be shown to exist and exactly against whom it may be asserted. Let's explore one possible answer to that question.

All of us are all born into some kind of economic system which may range from the relatively simple practices of primitive tribes to the complex transactions we find in highly industrialized, technology-oriented societies. While many of us could, if we had to, scratch out a living by farming, or hunting, or gathering, most of us in the highly industrialized countries, at least, get our access to material resources by way of a "job" (using the term in its widest sense to include all occupations and professions), by "work." There are, of course, people who don't need a job because they depend on the work of others, they live on their investments or have inherited wealth, or they are physically or psychologically unable to work.

I argued earlier that every human being has a moral right to acquire and use some share of material resources to insure living at a decent level of physical and psychological well-being, and it seems to follow that if most people are subject to an economic system in which a job is the means by which they obtain resources, then they have a moral right to a job; the economic system owes them employment. One weakness of this argument as stated is that a society can, through its economic system, insure that everyone enjoys some minimal level of material prosperity without providing everyone with a job, through various forms of welfare programs. But the argument is strengthened if its premises include the proposition that our sense of worth as human beings depends on our making a contribution to our own and our family's and society's well-being, which depends, in turn, on our doing it through a job (R. DeGeorge, 1990). In the abstract, then, it sounds like a case can be made for a moral right to employment, but we need to expose what that means in concrete terms, in the actual circumstances and conditions of a particular economic system. The "system," after all, is just a handy collective term of reference to the myriad individual economic transactions going on every day among the members of a particular society.

In a capitalistic economic system like our own in the United States, the private sector of the economy provides most job opportunities, so the thrust of the argument for a moral right to employment appears to fall on private employers. In effect, are all industries and businesses morally obligated to employ some minimum number of people to achieve a satisfactory level of employment in the society in which they operate?

The answer seems to be "no," if that society has adopted as its preferred economic system one whose very nature requires extensive freedom for its commercial enterprises in order to generate a maximum level of material prosperity for its members. In the capitalistic system, this freedom includes the right to hire and keep on the payroll only those employees needed to meet the demands for a particular business's products and to operate efficiently at a satisfactory level of profit. It also seems to include taking on only those people whose education, skills, and personality traits are judged best suited to the operations the business engages in.

One very large assumption being made here is that the option to live under the capitalistic system can be shown to be freely chosen by the members of a society either through some direct democratic process or by the notion of an implicit social contract among them. In other words, by continuing to live under the system without political protest, they indirectly indicate their preference for it. Given this assumption, the freedom of employers to hire and retain employees as they see fit entails that no member of the society in which they operate has a moral claim on any specific job offered in the private sector.

Because the capitalistic economic system responds as it does to market forces affecting levels of employment, it cannot guarantee a job to everyone who wants one, at least not on any long-term, continuous basis. There will likely always be those people whose particular skills, for whatever reason, simply are not needed by any business enterprise. Based on the arguments offered here, it may be true that they have no moral right to any specific job in any business, but they still have a right to work. Their society, then, which has decided on a capitalistic economic system has an obligation to provide them with work through its political structure. Welfare programs by themselves are not enough. This means that the government may need to provide training in advanced skills for those who lose their jobs because they cannot cope with the sophisticated technology required in today's employment market. Government may even have to offer jobs as the "employer of last resort." These jobs have to be more than just "make-work"; they should be directed at meaningful kinds of public service not easily provided by the private sector like rebuilding and constructing transportation facilities; building parks, campgrounds and public monuments; or working in libraries and health-care institutions.

The funds for all these functions have to come from some form of tax on those who own, work for, and are retired from viable economic enterprises. These people have a right to use natural resources for their own benefit, but their right to the yield of these resources is not exclusive because, in light of the earlier arguments I offered for entitlement to natural resources, some of the productive potential of those same resources belongs to the people who are unemployed through no fault of their own.

FAIR HIRING PRACTICES

Take a hypothetical case where one or the other of an employment agency's client companies ask the agency not to send minority candidates to them for job interviews because they prefer to hire people who fit a certain profile, white, blond, blue-eyed, and good-looking, who fit the corporate "front-office image." May these companies argue that since no individual person has any moral claim on the jobs they are offering, they have a right to employ whomever they wish—even if that means establishing discriminatory criteria that are not job-related?

The natural-law moralist (or anyone committed to a rights-based moral theory) would point out that while there is no positive duty to hire a particular individual for a specific job, screening practices based on race, gender, age, or religious preference violate the right of everyone to be treated with the dignity due a human person and are immoral. Consequently, employers have a negative duty not to discriminate on characteristics that have nothing to do with performing the job. Utilitarians, I think, would come to the same conclusion, although their judgment would, of course, depend on weighing the consequences these practices would produce on the whole. Cultural relativists would decide that if there were no laws against discrimination, hiring and promotion policies would follow whatever customs were acceptable in society. Many employers, for example, probably appealed to "community standards" to justify not hiring or promoting black people prior to the 1960s civil rights legislation.

Are the employment agencies morally wrong if they comply with discriminatory practices and refuse to send minority or other applicants on interviews for positions they are qualified to fill? Is an agency's cooperation formal or material in this instance? I believe that the natural-law moralist would consider it formal since the agencies have agreed to become an extension of a client's employment office and are performing a direct act of discrimination that is morally wrong in itself. The utilitarian, on the other hand, would likely want to weigh the consequences for the agency if it should lose clients by a refusal to cooperate in discriminatory practices and try to determine whether or not a better state of affairs would result overall from complying with them. The cultural relativist would approve compliance with an employer's wishes if discrimination were an accepted social practice and not against the law.

AFFIRMATIVE ACTION AND PREFERENTIAL TREATMENT

There are many interpretations of just what "affirmative action" means. The approach to this effort may range all the way from setting specific numbers of minorities to be moved into positions over a given time period so that the proportion of the positions they hold begins to approach their numerical distribution in the general population, to establishing the overall principle that employment and promotion opportunities are open to all, regardless of gender, race, religion, age, or disabled status.

It's very likely that both natural-law and utilitarian moralists would agree that everyone should have an equal opportunity to compete for any job he or she is qualified to do and would endorse this sense of affirmative action. Cultural relativists, again, would fall back on society's customary practices and wouldn't agree to the idea of equal opportunity just on its face. But what about preferential treatment (popularly referred to as "setting quotas"), the practice of hiring or promoting members of minority groups in preference to those from nonminority groups?

One rationale for this practice is to redress past injustices committed by American industry and government agencies in their hiring and promotion practices against blacks, women, hispanics, American Indians and any other minority groups. It is designed to insure that members of minority groups are represented in the offices and opportunities a society has to offer in proportion to their numbers in society.

But while the fact of past discrimination is not disputed, this particular remedy for it often is. The key rebuttal against preferential treatment centers on the contention that the person who receives it is not, in most cases, at least, the person who suffered the injustice, and the person (usually a white male) who is being passed over for a position or office because of the preferential treatment being given to a member of a minority group is not the one who committed the injustice in the first place. Therefore, the argument goes, preferential hiring and promotion commit the very offense they are supposed to remedy, namely, selection of a person purely on the basis of some characteristic which has nothing to do with performing a function or job. Setting specific numerical quotas for minorities is, on this view, just plain immoral. What needs to be implemented is a going-forward policy of equal opportunity, selecting people just on their qualifications for a position.

One reply to this argument, offered by Daniel Maguire, claims that its premise exonerating white males is false. While a particular white male may not have directly discriminated against a minority person, he shares in a kind of collective guilt on the part of his society that has failed to care enough or do enough to stop past discrimination. Further, some of these acts of discrimination have quite likely benefited him personally. On Maquire's view, we must render to others what they deserve in legal justice, the debt we owe to the common good by virtue of our social personhood. He thinks that invidious American individualism has blinded us to this social obligation; we confuse justice with equality when we should be concerned with justice as fairness. We focus incorrectly on the kind of justice that governs interpersonal transactions among equals instead of on distributive and legal justice that govern interrelationships among members of a community. Therefore, while affirmative action quotas as a remedy for legal and distributive injustice may be unequal, they are not unfair (Maguire, 1977).

I suspect that many Americans would not accept Maguire's argument, especially if they have tried to influence legislators to outlaw discriminatory practices in the marketplace, or have worked diligently within the limits of their own authority in the business world to hire and promote people from minority groups. They would likely resist the idea that they shared in a collective guilt for discrimination and, if passed over for a particular position just because they were white males, would deeply resent the explanation that they were simply paying the price for their past sins.

Maguire refers to St. Thomas Aquinas' contention that the community, not just the ruler, is where distributive justice resides, is its subject, and that the members of the community are "pleased and satisfied with a just distribution" (St. Thomas Aquinas, 1952). Aquinas suggests that a particular member of the community may have an obligation to be sure that another individual or family is receiving a just share of the community's goods. This means, if I understand him correctly, that even as individuals we are responsible for seeing the common good realized in our fellow community members' situations, and we may even have to give up something we have to insure that happens.

I would like to pick up on Aquinas' idea that the members of a community are pleased with a just distribution and give it my own extended interpretation as a possible rationale for preferential treatment in hiring and promotion.

Concretely, this abstract idea might mean that the people in a society, in "seeing" that members of its subgroups are proportionately represented in all its offices and positions, in the government, in business and industry, in the arts, in academia, and in sports see an affirmation of the value of human personhood that underlies all accidental differences in people. That affirmation should be regarded as a desirable social goal benefitting every individual member of society, and promoting that goal by means that rely on what are ordinarily irrelevant factors in the selection of individuals for offices and positions is not unjust because those factors are now relevant from the standpoint of effecting distributive justice. In the business world, for example, members of minority groups who come in contact with the people in higher levels of management derive a sense of contentment and affirmation of their own personhood when they see that they are "represented" in reasonable proportion in those levels—even if they acknowledge that they personally may not have the talent required to reach them. On this line of argument, then, preferential treatment may be the only way to establish the balance that should exist in these structures in a society, and are not unjust—any more, for example, than drafting a subgroup of young males to fight a society's wars is considered unjust discrimination.

Natural-law moralists might arrive at different conclusions on preferential hiring and promotion depending on how they see justice at work in the practice. The idea of social rather than commutative justice might persuade some of them that this practice is morally justified. Others might see it as reverse discrimination, a violation of the rights of individuals who were not responsible for past social injustice. Or they might argue that it is simply a case of selection of people for a position on irrelevant grounds, an act of disrespect for the people who were passed over in the process and morally wrong in itself.

The utilitarian moralist's approach to preferential treatment would, of course, be to predict the overall good and bad consequences that would result from the practice. If it appeared that it would generate more good than bad consequences on the whole, then it would be morally required— even if individual white males would have to be passed over for positions they were clearly qualified for. These white males would not be able to claim that they had been treated unfairly.

The cultural relativist would try to determine whether society approved or disapproved of preferential treatment, either by law or custom, and act accordingly.

The basic principle governing hiring and promotion for both natural-law and utilitarian moralists is, I believe, that in the overall interest of society's well-being, managers are obliged to stick to qualifications alone in their selections for jobs and promotions unless a persuasive case has been made for instituting and following preferential treatment for some determinate period of time. (Cultural relativists will fall back on society's practices in this matter.) Does that mean managers must flip a coin, so to speak, when several equally-qualified candidates—e.g., black, hispanic, female, white male—present themselves for a position? In an extreme situation, that might be a reasonable thing to do, but choices in these cases are ordinarily justified in some minimal way, such as by deciding that one applicant is better than the others because he or she has better communication skills or would be easier to work with and, consequently, would be more likely to contribute to the smooth operation of the enterprise. It would probably even be morally acceptable to hire or promote a fully-qualified relative or friend, since no one individual applicant has any prima facie title to the position under consideration.

WAGES

Employees' wages are generally determined by the market: whatever it takes to attract and keep productive people. In larger industries, it is commonly assumed that competitive salaries include basic wages and bonuses plus assorted benefits like paid holidays, vacations, sick days, medical and dental insurance, and savings and pension plans. In smaller businesses, wages are very often simply a function or what an enterprise can afford; benefits may or may not be a part of the package.

What wages are employees morally entitled to? Are they entitled to a certain level of benefits in addition to a basic wage? Their employment, as was argued earlier, is their access to their fair share of material resources, so at a minimum it seems that their jobs must provide them with wages and benefits at a level that will assure their living in some minimal but decent set of conditions. That appears to be the rationale, for example, behind the federal minimum hourly wage in certain job categories. What is clear, I think, is that shareholders and company officers have no right to a disproportionate share of a company's revenues if that forces employees and their families to accept levels of wages and benefits that won't suffice to support them at a decent human level of existence.

Not every business may be able to afford this ideal. Does this mean that those that can't because they simply aren't big enough should be required to go out of business on moral grounds, grounds of justice? At least two practical reasons, I think, argue against it. First, small enterprises provide a living for their owners, at least (think of "mom and pop" kinds of establishments). Second, they likely employ many people who lack the education and skills needed to work in larger and more sophisticated industries. Low-paying jobs may well be the financial stopgap these workers need until they can acquire the skills that will get them into better-paying jobs. Or it may be the case that they are the second wage earner in a family and want this income just to supplement the family's minimal living requirements until the principal wage earner has a job that takes care of them. In any case, since it isn't possible to require a particular business to pay wages larger than it can legitimately afford, what these people can't earn toward their minimally decent standard of living needs to come from the government as a matter of distributive justice. That amount will be based on appropriate economic statistics, such as "what it takes to sustain a family of four."

SOME MORE THOUGHTS ABOUT WAGES

Equal Pay for Equal Work

The principle "equal pay for equal work" is currently established as part of U.S. labor law. People performing the same kind of work must be paid the same salaries unless the fact that some of them can do the work faster or more efficiently because they have been at it longer than other, newer, employees justifies paying them more. Race, gender, age, and handicaps have no bearing on pay treatment where equal work is concerned.

Does social justice require that employees with dependents, families to support, for example, should be paid more than people with no dependents but who are doing the exact same work? It seems like a case could be made for that requirement if a person's dependents gain their rightful access to resources solely through his or her work efforts. It is unlikely, however, that such disparate treatment would ever be accepted in the United States. Single people would surely argue that an employer only has to pay the market wage for a particular job and is not in the business of caring for social justice. They might argue further that the person with dependents probably freely chose to found a family and spend his or her income that way instead of on sports cars, expensive vacations, or high living in general. He or she does not have a right to a subsidy for that life-style choice, a subsidy derived from paying lower salaries to coworkers without such obligations. If distributive justice is at issue, they might argue, it constitutes an obligation falling on society in general; special welfare or family-subsidy programs may well be called for but they should be a responsibility shared by everyone in the community on some equitable basis.

In the United States, at least for many years, this issue did not arise because the productivity and general financial success of large enterprises allowed them to pay the same level of wages and benefits to all employees doing the same kind of work and those with dependents earned enough to care for them decently. The size and profit levels of smaller businesses probably would never be enough to try to pay their employees with dependents anything other than the going market rates, so government would have to provide those people with some sort of family subsidy.

Equal Pay for Comparable Work

In recent years the notion of "equal pay for comparable worth" or work has influenced some states in the United States to require paying people in government jobs having widely different content (tree trimmers and typists, perhaps) the same salaries if it can be demonstrated that these jobs require the same relative levels of education, skill, knowledge, and experience. The spur for this approach to establishing salaries was the incontrovertible fact that for years women were paid lower wages for many kinds of work that required the same skills and knowledge demanded in jobs held by men who were paid higher wages for doing them.

Is equal pay for comparable work a requirement of justice? One business ethicist, Richard DeGeorge, argues that it is not. He thinks that the market is still the most efficient allocator of jobs because even though skill and knowledge requirements may look the same for many jobs, other factors (probably like long hours, risk or physical environment) have to be considered. What is morally required is that no class of people may be excluded from obtaining these higher-paying jobs on irrelevant grounds. If females have been traditionally excluded from them just because they were female, that discriminatory practice has to be discontinued (R. DeGeorge, 1990).

I think DeGeorge makes a good case.

WHO GETS WHAT SHARE OF THE RETURN
ON RESOURCES?

There is probably some relationship between the amount of material resources a company uses and its obligation to distribute the return realized from those resources to society's members. What that return is, of course, doesn't depend solely on the amount of resources used, but also on how well a company manages them and how productive its workers are. Managers and workers, then, have a right to a fair share of the return in proportion to their contribution to the enterprise's success, with emphasis on the word "fair." Top managers usually think that they make the biggest contribution and as a result expect the biggest relative share of the wages and bonuses paid by the enterprise. In some cases, however, their salaries and perks often appear to be, to the social justice sceptic at least, a disproportionate share of a company's total compensation package.

Shareholders, of course, have a right to a fair share of their companies' return. Some people might argue that as the owners of the business, they have first claim on the return and the right to the largest relative share. The shareholders, however, through their investment in companies, are simply accessing resources and are entitled, like everybody else, to a fair share of the return on those resources. "Fair" in this case certainly includes compensation for the risk taken in making those investments, but it does not include compensation that might depend on paying substandard wages or benefits to employees.

SUMMARY

If good managers want to hire and retain productive and loyal employees, they need to offer them competitive salaries and benefits, training, a say in how jobs are structured and what their short and long-term objectives will be, adequate feedback on performance, opportunities for promotion in the business, a way to appeal perceived injustices without fear of reprisal, and safe working conditions. These practices are part of good management, but they have a moral dimension as well because failure to implement them may do an injustice or injury to a person or diminish his or her dignity.

In this chapter, we examined employment rights and some thoughts about just wages. Since people depend on an economic system to provide for their needs and contribute to society, it can be argued that the economic system owes everyone a job. In a capitalistic system, freely accepted by a society's members, a business hires and retains only the number of people it needs to operate efficiently and profitably. No business is obliged to guarantee a job to anyone it doesn't need on the payroll.

If private enterprise can't insure jobs for everybody who needs one, the government has to step in with training in new skills, where that's appropriate, or employment on meaningful government projects. Temporary welfare programs like unemployment compensation are not enough.

Managers and their agents are obliged to follow fair hiring practices, avoiding discrimination against people on grounds of gender, race, age, or disabled status when those characteristics are irrelevant to the job to be done. Natural-law moralists would see such discrimination as morally wrong in itself because it is a violation of the respect due to human beings and their right to work. Utilitarians would judge any discriminatory practices on the basis of the net good or bad consequences they produce on the whole. The cultural relativist would follow the hiring and promotion practices or laws endorsed by society.

Affirmative action poses a particularly thorny issue when it is interpreted as "quota setting", as an attempt to insure that members of groups that have suffered discrimination in the past are represented in the opportunities society has to offer roughly in proportion to their numbers in the community. These people are treated "preferentially," hired and promoted over members of traditional groups like white males. Some theorists see this practice as an affirmation of "personhood" in that people would see "their kind" represented in all levels of the positions business, for one, has to offer. Some would see it as a requirement of distributive justice, arguing that all of us in society are collectively guilty of tolerating this kind of discrimination in the past, and, in the case of white males, at least, benefitting by it.

One key argument against preferential treatment is that it commits the very offense it intends to redress: discrimination, but in reverse. It makes choices on the irrelevant grounds of race, gender, age, or disabled status. Another argument is that the person who is passed over in the selection process is most likely not the one who did the discriminating in the past, and the person who receives preferential treatment is not usually the one who was discriminated against. These arguments turn on the idea that commutative justice which governs transactions between individuals is violated. A counter argument is that distributive justice governing the distribution of society's goods and offices among its members overrides claims in commutative justice and justifies preferential treatment both in hiring and promotion.

Natural-law moralists would likely approve or disapprove of preferential treatment on the basis of whether they saw it satisfying distributive justice or violating commutative justice. Utilitarians would want to weigh up the good and bad consequences of the practice to see which would prevail.

The cultural relativist would want to determine whether society approved or disapproved of it either by customary practice or as a matter of law.

In examining the issue of wages, we saw that people need to earn enough to care for their human needs at some comfortable level. That would define a minimally just wage, and a business seems obliged to pay it. Where businesses—simply because they aren't big enough—can't pay a basic wage and all the benefit packages we have grown accustomed to seeing offered by large industries, the government may have to step in with some kind of supplemental welfare package for their employees to insure that all of them are living in humane conditions.

"Equal pay for equal work" is a matter of law now, but recently, the concept of "equal pay for comparable work" has become popular because women, historically, have predominated in many lower-paying jobs that demand the same level of skills, knowledge, training, and experience as many men's jobs. If the job requirements are the same, the argument goes, the pay should be the same—no matter how much the actual kind of work done may differ. Opponents of this concept argue that it interferes with the efficiency of the marketplace and ignores other conditions about some jobs like long hours or severe safety hazards that may require better pay. Justice only requires that women need to have access on an equal opportunity basis to these kinds of jobs.

We touched on the question of who has what rights to the return on resources. Managers and workers have a claim to a fair share in proportion to their efforts to use resources efficiently and productively. Shareholders have the right to a return on their resources consistent with the risks they take, but their rights to a return do not outweigh the workers' rights to a decent wage.

NOTE

1. Tomasko, R. M. "The Right Way to Shrink a Company, *The New York Times,* January 10, 1988, Sec. 4, p. 3. Copyright © 1988 by The New York Times Company. Reprinted by permission.

7

Employee Privacy

RESPECTING EMPLOYEES' RIGHTS TO PRIVACY

Any company has a right to protect itself from fraud, loss of its proprietary information and trade secrets, and from harm to its facilities, employees, customers, or to the public it serves. Since employees are one potential source of these harms, managers would like to know something about a job applicant's personal history: was he or she ever fired by a previous employer for alcohol or other substance abuse? Was he or she ever fired for or convicted of theft? Some companies use preemployment tests to get a reading on a person's honesty; polygraph tests, for example, although now illegal for that purpose, were used in the past by many companies as a preemployment screening device. Managers may also want to monitor and even attempt to restrict the private-life activities of people already on the payroll to be sure that they do not constitute some kind of threat to the business. But just how far may managers invade a prospective or current employee's privacy in the interests of the enterprise? Does a company's right to protect itself always override an employee's right to privacy?

It was reported, a few years ago, that I.B.M. fired a manager for dating a manager in a rival firm. The company saw the relationship as a conflict of interest (Brophy, 1985).

Is a company morally justified in firing an employee in a case like this? Let's speculate. Since the person she was dating worked for a rival firm, her company was obviously afraid that she might pass him, however inadvertently, proprietary information. It probably seemed that the only way to insure this wouldn't happen was to demand that she end the relationship or that, perhaps, she should accept a different position in the company, one that didn't deal with sensitive information that might be useful to the other firm. The company could have argued that it was not interfering with her right to continue seeing this person; it was only insisting that she had to choose between her interest in him and her present position with the company. If, of course, the company wouldn't offer her another position or she would have refused that option, the situation would boil down to a choice between her friend and her job.

The right to choose one's friends including someone who might turn out to be a potential marriage partner is so basic that it seems to lie outside the legitimate concern of an employer. In this case, I think the company would have every right to raise the issue with this manager, point out the concern over safeguarding proprietary information, and then let her clearly understand that if she should violate her trust and pass on any of the company's marketing or other secrets to any unauthorized person, let alone her friend, she would be liable to disciplinary action—including the possibility of losing her job altogether. It is very common today for all employees in a company to sign a formal agreement to that effect, and very few employees think it an unwarranted intrusion on their privacy. But to require her to stop seeing this person as a condition of keeping her present position would, it seems to me, be just such an intrusion.

Let's speculate further. Could she have made a promise to stop seeing her friend and then resume the relationship on the grounds that she could not be bound by a morally illegitimate condition for employment?

The utilitarian moralist would require that she weigh the possible consequences of her action and decide whether the total good for everybody would outweigh the harm that might result. It's likely that a promise like that could turn out to produce more potentially harmful consequences than good ones, and she would be advised not to make it. Her reputation for trustworthiness could be destroyed in the company's eyes, if the company found out what she had done, and her future advancement—if not her job—would be jeopardized. The company might need to make costly changes in its administrative or marketing strategies since it couldn't be sure that some of them hadn't been compromised by this relationship. The details of the situation might even get passed on to her friend's company, and his reputation and job could also be jeopardized.

A natural-law moralist would hold that making a false promise, telling a lie, in effect, is intrinsically wrong and could not be done, although it might be argued that if the company had no moral right to exact that kind of promise, the employee could be justified in making a kind of "mental reservation," that is, withholding part of the truth by limiting the meaning of what she said in some way and hoping her employer wouldn't pick up the clue to that limited meaning. She might say something like: "I'll just remain good friends with him," hoping the company would be satisfied with its own understanding of what "good friends" meant. But I think it would be hard for a natural-law moralist to defend the mental reservation solution here because of the seriousness of the consequences for the company and for her if her strategem were discovered. The company, in its own defense, would have to make changes in strategies and plans that it suspected might have been compromised—a costly procedure. Her career with the company would surely be jeopardized. Finally, she was likely talented enough to get another job somewhere else or, even if she were moved to some other position in the company, probably had the potential to move up on some other track.

A cultural relativist would require her to determine whether any law applied in this case, and if not, what society's customs dictated. If society in general thought that no one should be expected to make this kind of promise or should make it in her own interest but not keep it, she would have done the morally right thing. But if it was expected, in her culture, that promises like this one should be kept, she would have done something morally wrong. Since, in the case cited, a court awarded the manager a significant sum as damages (Brophy), it looks like a cultural relativist could conclude that society disapproves of any company's invading an employee's privacy in matters like this.

SUBSTANCE ABUSE

None of us wants to put his or her life in the hands of anyone whose ability to function is impaired by alcohol or other drugs. We want train engineers, airline pilots, taxi drivers, bus drivers, and the like to be alert and capable of operating their machines safely. We expect doctors and nurses and other health-care givers to function at a fully professional level all the time. No company wants to be placed in jeopardy by employees who can't perform their duties because they are high on some kind of drug or are drunk.

Because of the widespread abuse of alcohol and other drugs today, many employers fear they may unwittingly hire an addict or alcoholic. Consequently, testing for drug use is a preemployment requirement in many businesses. Do companies have a moral right to insist on such testing?

The right not to have one's privacy invaded is not absolute in the sense that a person may never waive it. In the interest of showing a potential employer that he or she is not a possible threat to the business, a job applicant may certainly agree to being tested for drugs. Likewise, it seems evident that a company is morally justified in insisting on testing job applicants for drug use as a protective measure, especially where the safety of customers and employees is at stake. The company requiring the tests, however, needs to insure that the tests are accurate (including providing subsequent tests if the results of the first one are positive), that the applicant is permitted to furnish evidence that he or she is taking drugs under a legitimate medical prescription, and that the results of the tests remain confidential and will be made known only to those people in the company who have a need to see them. If these precautions cannot be reasonably observed, then the company has no right to demand these tests.

What about testing people already on the payroll? The principle of "probable cause" seems applicable, meaning that testing for drug abuse is legitimate only if an employer has a valid suspicion that a person's work performance is being adversely affected by drug use. That means training supervisors in proper techniques of recognizing the signs of abuse. It may also mean testing "after the fact," if an employee has been involved in an incident that has harmed others or has caused extensive property damage. It's small comfort, of course, to find out that an employee was high on drugs or drunk after he or she may have caused an airline, train, or bus accident in which people were killed or injured. That unhappy conclusion explains why employers want to resort to random testing of all employees in occupations where the risk of harm to people or property is high if these employees make a mistake.

Is random testing of employees morally justified? It seems to me that only two circumstances could justify any testing of employees: valid suspicion that a particular employee is on drugs or statistically valid evidence that the incidence of drug use in the employee body is significant. It would be particularly applicable in jobs where the safety of other employees, customers, or the general public would be threatened by impaired job performance. Equality of persons would appear to require that all employees in the population should be tested, but that could be an extremely costly effort. If random testing insures satisfactory results, it seems that it is morally justified as long as all employees in the population are equally subject to it.

ABUSING EMPLOYEES

It is probably not uncommon for bosses to fly into rages at their subordinates, berating them at meetings in front of other employees. Employees may even be threatened with the loss of their jobs for such failures as not agreeing to fudge financial statements, refusing sexual advances, not trying to get out of jury duty, or refusing to commit perjury on behalf of a union or company.

I think such instances involve clear violations of privacy. It is certainly necessary to let an employee know that he or she is not performing satisfactorily, but that is not something other employees or managers who are not in the person's direct line of supervision or who will not likely ever supervise that person have a right to know. Everyone is entitled to his or her good public reputation. No one may be subjected to unwanted sexual proposals; his or her person is private. Finally, using threats to try to force employees to violate the law is a kind of invasion of privacy: it intrudes on the realm of conscience and puts the person in legal jeopardy.

For the natural-law or any rights-based moralist, all of these instances are evidence of employee abuse, of violations of human dignity, respect for persons and, therefore, are immoral. And it's hard to see how any utilitarian calculus could ever support the conclusion that these practices would produce more good consequences on the whole and could be justified morally. As for cultural relativism, I doubt that mores anywhere in the United States would dictate accepting this kind of treatment in the workplace.

SUMMARY

Companies want to protect themselves, their employees, and their customers from avoidable harm. As a result, they believe that they need to know about the personal histories and habits of their employees to guard against fraud, theft of proprietary information or harmful acts employees might perform under the influence of alcohol or other drugs. Does a company have a right, in its own interests, to this kind of information or is it an unwarranted intrusion on employees' privacy?

We noted one case where a company intervened in an intimate personal relationship of a manager, firing her because it saw her dating a manager in a competing company as a conflict of interest—meaning, probably, that the company feared she might pass on to her friend, perhaps inadvertently, proprietary information.

It was argued that the company had gone too far here, that at most her supervisor should have discussed the situation with her and warned her that any unwarranted transfer of sensitive information to anybody could result in her being fired.

We also looked at whether she might be justified in telling her employer that she had broken off the relationship knowing full well that she intended to continue it on the grounds that the company had no business intervening in her personal life in the first place. It appeared that the natural-law moralist would have regarded this as a lie, and that even a "mental reservation," a half-truth, in effect, would be morally questionable in this instance because, if she were found out, the company would have to make costly changes in any strategies or plans it thought might have been compromised, and her own career in the business would be threatened. The utilitarian would likely predict that more bad than good consequences would result from this line of action, both for herself and the company if her deception were found out.

A cultural relativist would probably be right to suggest that the mores in the United States, at least, would not approve of the company's action in a case like this. A court decision made in this person's favor against the company offered support for that judgment.

On the issue of testing for substance abuse, it seems that in government agencies and industries where employees whose judgment and motor skills are impaired by alcohol or drugs may do serious harm to people and property, such testing can be justified morally. Companies are obliged, however, to insure that test results are valid before acting on them, and have to respect an employee's right to privacy here. Random testing for substance abuse seems morally acceptable where there is strong evidence that a significant number of employees may be abusing alcohol or using illegal drugs or where employee and public safety is at issue. Equality of persons requires that all employees in the population are equally subject to be tested randomly.

Berating employees in public for poor work performance is a violation of their privacy. Everyone has a right to his or her public reputation, and only those who need to know about a person's questionable performance should hear about it. Threatening a person for refusing to do something immoral or illegal invades a person's conscience or puts him or her in legal jeopardy and is a violation of privacy. Sexual advances violate an individual's private person.

Natural-law moralists would regard any abuse of an employee as morally wrong, and utilitarians, I think, would find it justified only in extreme circumstances where the overall good somehow demanded it. Cultural relativists would have to determine whether the particular community where it was occurring would tolerate it.

8

Performance Appraisals

RANKING AND RATING

How well employees are paid ordinarily depends on how well their supervisors think they are doing their jobs. And, while performance on the job and potential for advancement are not the same thing, a person who may be able to handle increased responsibility probably won't move up in the business without performing well in a current assignment.

All employees are subject to some kind of performance appraisal, formal or informal. In small business operations, owner-bosses generally can observe the performance of employees directly, and the appraisal process is not very complex. Large companies, particularly those with many people in management pay grades, rank and rate the people in various units of the business against their peers. Employees who are considered better performers than the other people at the same level in the unit should get better salary treatment.

Take a hypothetical case where the supervisors in a particular organization ranked and rated their subordinates and then proposed what they thought was appropriate merit salary treatment for each of them. The department head who had to approve the merit salary treatment rejected their recommendations and directed them to move a manager who had been ranked about midway among his peers to the top rank.

The department head had been impressed with this individual's communication skills, and he believed that fact justified the change. Although the supervisors in the unit argued that this manager's ranking was based strictly on performance, in accordance with the provisions of the company's appraisal plan, the department head overruled them and awarded him the top merit salary treatment. Was justice violated in this situation?

Suppose a second case where a large corporation's efficiency measurement plan did not fit a particular manager's operation—through no fault of the manager. The manager's performance rating was downgraded because her results did not meet the objectives set under the plan. Subsequently, the plan's structure was corrected to allow for the special situation in which she was operating, and her efficiency results suddenly became outstanding. Was this manager's treatment unethical prior to the change in the measurement plan?

ETHICAL IMPLICATIONS FOR PERFORMANCE APPRAISALS

People express their dignity and worth as persons through their work; it provides them with a means to achieve personal goals and contribute to their own, their families', and society's well-being. I believe that the formal or informal public recognition their work receives from the various communities to which they belong is a powerful constituent of their self-image, of "who they are," and no opinion is more immediately important to them than how their bosses think they are doing.

Managers have a duty to prepare sound performance appraisals. If employees are not reasonably sure that their pay treatment is fair, their morale and performance will suffer. But there is also a moral dimension to this responsibility on two counts. First, there is the impact appraisals have on the persons being evaluated, on their perception of their self-worth as measured by what their supervisors think of them. Second, the company's appraisal plan that outlines the ground rules for preparing performance evaluations constitutes a moral contract with employees because it is a promise; it ordinarily stipulates that how well an individual meets the standards established in the plan will determine how much he or she will be paid. A supervisor who fails to follow the appraisal plan acts unjustly toward subordinates who have a right to be judged in line with its provisions and standards.

A FEW KEY ETHICAL DOS AND DON'TS FOR PERFORMANCE APPRAISALS

To insure ethical treatment of employees in the appraisal process, some fundamental dos and don'ts need to be observed. While the following guidelines may seem to be nothing more than good management skills that can be found described in any basic management textbook, they have moral force because they affect human beings whose dignity requires that they be treated justly and with the respect due them as persons:

- Subordinates need to have clear and concrete objectives set out for the appraisal period, and they need to provide their own input to these objectives. Respect for their autonomy demands that they have a chance to exercise control over their life circumstances—including, to a reasonable extent, their jobs.

- Employees have a right to feedback on their performance on some regular basis. It would be unfair, for example, to wait until the end of the appraisal period to tell someone that he or she was performing at a poor or unsatisfactory level.

- Performance must be measured by valid criteria. It would be unjust to knowingly measure a person's performance using a plan which did not apply in some significant respect to the operation being managed and unfairly indicated that the manager was not competent.

- Supervisors need to bring adequate anecdotal information on a subordinate's accomplishments and failures to ranking and rating sessions. Bosses who fail to make a respectable case for subordinates by relying on half-remembered details from incidents occurring during the appraisal period may cause their people to lose out in the competition for merit salary treatment with their peers whose bosses can cite chapter and verse on their performances.

- A subordinate whose performance is poor or unsatisfactory has to be made aware of that fact. That is part of a boss's job responsibility. It would be unkind and unjust to let a person think he or she is doing a good job when that is not the case. Subordinates have a right to counseling, coaching, and training from their bosses when that kind of help will improve performance. If it is clear that a particular individual is in over his or her head in an assignment, that it is clearly beyond his or her skills, the boss has a moral duty, out of respect for the person, to convey that fact and, even, perhaps, to help find a position where he or she can be successful. (If, of course, no job can be found for this person anywhere in the company, he or she has to be fired.)

- Only those people who have had sufficient contact with a person's performance should have a say in its appraisal. Higher-level managers sometimes believe that they have developed special insights and intuitions which enable them to make immediate judgments about individuals based on casual encounters with them or brief observations of their work, but I believe that claim to be highly suspect. These executives are bound to listen carefully to the recommendations of the supervisors who have had regular contact with the people being evaluated, and, unless there are grounds to suspect that one or the other appraisal has been poorly done, the executives need to respect judgments made by these supervisors.

To return to the two cases described earlier, in the case where the department head moved an individual from the middle to the top of the ranking list, a utilitarian might try to make the case that better consequences overall would result from encouraging a talented individual who might do more for the company in the long run. A rights-oriented moralist, however, would likely argue that it was unjust to the individual who had earned that top rank based on a performance that was judged according to the appraisal plan's guidelines and standards. In the second case, where a manager's performance was downgraded because of a flawed measurement plan, justice was violated if the evaluators knew about the plan's weaknesses. It was also an affront to the manager's dignity as a person because it damaged her self-image by implying that she was not a good manager. A utilitarian moralist might think that overall, worse consequences would result for the business and other supervisors if the plan's weaknesses became generally known and that the unfair evaluation of the manager should be allowed to stand. I suspect, however, that even a utilitarian would come to the conclusion that more overall harm would be done by an unfair evaluation in this case; the morale and performance of other supervisors would likely suffer if they found out about this supervisor's treatment and thought they might be treated in the same way someday. Their confidence in higher management's integrity would surely be shaken, to say the least.

The cultural relativist would look to whatever laws might apply to appraisal systems (regarding illegal discriminatory practices) or to what a society generally considers acceptable appraisal treatment. It might be the case that it is customary for employers to always have the final say over whether and how employee performance is to be judged. In that case, the employer's judgment is the measure of morality in appraisals.

SUMMARY

How well employees are paid usually depends on how well they are rated by their bosses. Also, they ordinarily won't move up to higher positions of responsibility in the business unless they're performing well in current assignments.

All employees are subject to a formal or, certainly in small business operations, informal appraisal process. Large companies customarily establish ranking and rating systems that compare peers in a unit of the business and award merit pay treatment to those who are judged to be doing better jobs and contributing more.

We looked at a hypothetical case where a department head overrode the merit ranking established by the supervisors in a particular unit and moved a manager from the middle to the top spot in the ranking. The department head thought this manager's communication skills were better than the other managers', and that, as a result, he deserved better pay treatment.

In a second hypothetical case, we considered a situation where a manager's rating was downgraded not because she was a poor manager but because her efficiency results were dictated by a deficient measurement plan. When the plan's deficiencies were corrected, her results got better.

Performance appraisal systems have an ethical dimension. To start with, people express their dignity and worth through their work and provide for their own, their families' and even society's well-being. Formal and informal public recognition of their work, especially by their bosses, reaffirms their self-worth, their sense of "who they are."

Managers, then, have a moral, not just a managerial, obligation to prepare sound performance appraisals because of the impact they have on the people being evaluated, on their perception of their self-worth as measured by their bosses' opinions. In addition, the appraisal plan's ground rules constitute a moral contract with employees because it is a promise; it stipulates that a person will be judged and rewarded according to the standards set out in the plan.

Some key ethical dos and don'ts for appraisal plans were offered:

1. Subordinates have a right to have clear objectives set for the appraisal period and have a right to provide input to them as a way of exercising control over their lives.

2. Employees have a right to feedback on some regular basis. It would be unfair to wait until formal appraisal preparation time to tell someone he or she was not performing satisfactorily.

3. Performance must be measured by valid criteria. Applying deficient measurements to a manager's operation could unfairly indicate that he or she is not competent.

4. Supervisors need to bring adequate anecdotal information on subordinates to ranking and rating sessions. Otherwise, their subordinates will be at a disadvantage when other bosses present well-documented summaries of their people's performances.

5. A subordinate who is performing unsatisfactorily must be made aware of that fact and given counseling, coaching and training in an effort to help improve. If a particular assignment is over a person's head, he or she should be moved to one where he or she can be successful; if there is no place in the company where that can be accomplished, he or she will have to be fired.

6. Only people who have a good knowledge of what a person is doing should be allowed to rate his or her performance.

In the first case we looked at, it was suggested that a utilitarian might think that better long-range consequences for the business would result if a manager were moved up in the ranking based solely on his communication skills. A rights-based moralist would likely argue that it would be unjust to the individual who had earned the top spot based on a performance judged by the appraisal plan's standards.

In the second case, where a flawed measurement plan caused a downgrading in a manager's performance, justice was violated if the evaluators knew about the plan's weaknesses. Further, it violated the person's dignity by implying that she was not a good manager. A utilitarian moralist might think it better overall to let the evaluation stand for fear that the plan's weaknesses would become known to other managers. However, it seems that the morale and performance of other supervisors might suffer if they found out about the plan's weaknesses and realized that they could be treated in the same way some day.

The cultural relativist would look to whatever laws applied in appraisal situations or to whatever society found acceptable. It might be customary to let employers have the final say over whether and how people's performances are to be judged, and that judgment would then be the measure of morality in appraisal systems.

9

Firing Employees

WHEN MAY MANAGERS FIRE EMPLOYEES?

Consider this case reported in *The New York Times*:

> In May, 1989, a Federal Judge in Newark had found that Continental Can executives had violated Federal pension laws when they secretly had a computer program written that enabled the company to organize its work so that factories would be closed and workers laid off just before the workers became eligible for pension payments.[1]

Does a person, once hired, have a moral right to keep the job he or she was hired for? Earlier I argued that nobody has a moral claim on any specific job, so it would seem that nobody has a moral right to keep it once he or she is hired to do it. Past practice, in American business has been that any employee may be terminated "at will" unless a labor contract or other agreement covering the length of employment has been established. This practice has come under fire in the courts in recent years and is no longer regarded as an employer's absolute legal right (Arvanites and Ward, 1988).

THE NATURAL-LAW APPROACH

Let's see how a Natural-Law moralist, using the key concepts of justice and respect for human dignity, would likely look at the issue of firing employees.

If a particular job is no longer needed in a business operation, there is no moral obligation to retain it just to provide work for the person holding it. As we saw earlier, no company has a moral obligation to keep a certain minimum number of people employed just to satisfy the requirements of social justice; they can be cared for through the political system's governmental agencies. In fact, keeping employees on the payroll unnecessarily might unfairly reduce the owners' share of their company's revenues. Ordinarily, of course, it is to the company's advantage to keep productive and loyal employees in the operation, so good employees should be moved into available jobs requiring the same skill levels or be retrained for jobs requiring different skills.

If employees are meeting their job requirements at a fully satisfactory level, it seems that in virtue of their human dignity they should be kept on in those jobs as long as they are necessary to the operation. To terminate people, for example, because they exhibit offbeat personality traits that are not harmful to the business, because they have blown the whistle on questionable practices in the company, because they have resisted sexual advances, or because managers think others could do their jobs even better, would be clearly immoral.

When employees work for a company over a long period of time, they often develop strong psychological attachments to it. They obviously become used to the level of pay and benefits they enjoy and they identify with the company's "culture" which includes, among other features, the worth its product or service has for society, the way people are treated in the business, the long-term friendships that are made among the employees, and the way the company relates to the community at large. Termination, even "for cause," is a traumatic experience for them. To the extent that a company encourages long-term employment, for example, by giving raises tied to time on the job, by publicly acknowledging service anniversaries with gifts, by giving employees to understand that the longer they stay with the company the more the company values their work and their loyalty, and by holding out the promise of pension benefits, it establishes an implicit moral contract with employees to keep them on as long as they want to stay—always given the understanding that severe and permanent setbacks in the business's fortunes may require dismissing even long-term people. It would be immoral, on this account, for managers to dismiss long-term employees just before they become eligible for pensions or force them into early retirement in order to hire younger, less costly people for the same jobs as a way to reduce expenses and increase the return to the owners of the business. The owners have no right to a larger return at the expense of employees; they are bound to abide by the moral agreements, even implicit ones, made by the people they hire to run their businesses.

DISMISSAL FOR "JUST CAUSE"

Employees often have to fired because they can't or won't do their jobs in a satisfactory manner. The reasons for their failure may be varied: absenteeism, substance abuse, incompetence, or illegal behavior associated with their particular set of job responsibilities. Managers have a moral obligation to the owners of the business to insure that people who can't or won't perform are not kept on the payroll.

Some employees have a problem with chronic absenteeism: they can't be depended on to be at work when they are scheduled. The absence may not even be their fault; a debilitating illness over which they have no control may be the problem. Large companies ordinarily provide some kind of disability benefits in a good many of these cases, but there is a limit to how long they can pay them. When a valid health-care prognosis clearly indicates that an employee's health will never improve enough to allow him or her to return to the job, the company has no choice but dismissal. There is no moral requirement for it to assume long-term financial responsibility for employees in this situation unless their years of service entitle them to a disability pension and health insurance paid for by the company.

Companies are not required, morally, to keep people around who are chronically absent or fail to perform their jobs satisfactorily because of substance abuse. Large companies, realizing that they have made a substantial investment in hiring and training such employees, may offer them counseling and rehabilitation services, but I don't see that they are morally required to. Certainly, when it is clear that an employee's performance isn't improving, even with support from the company, he or she ought to be dismissed.

Employees who simply cannot do the job to which they are assigned because they don't have the intelligence or skills it demands may have to be demoted, and, if there is no other job in the company they can handle, fired. It is true that some manager at one time or other decided that this person could do the job, so the company has some responsibility for the situation. Respect for this employee as a person requires, I think, that supervision first make a serious attempt to help him or her by coaching or more training, but if that fails, the employee should be let go.

Supervisors may demote or fire, without any moral qualms, employees who commit illegal acts in the context of their job responsibilities, unless their actions were explicitly or implicitly approved by their supervisors, or unless some significantly extenuating circumstance (like previous long years of honest service) is a sufficient reason for more lenient treatment.

Respect for human dignity requires that employees who are let go for chronic absenteeism or poor job performance, or because the company is in serious financial straits, need to be given adequate notice of what will happen to them. They have a right to some time to absorb the shock of dismissal and look for new jobs or plan new careers. Long-term employees, of course, are entitled to any pension benefits they have earned. Severance pay is probably not a moral requirement unless it has been agreed to as a condition of employment.

THE UTILITARIAN APPROACH

The utilitarian moralist has to weigh the consequences for both the company and the individual when deciding whether or not to fire someone. The effect on the company that keeps an unproductive employee on the payroll or one who doesn't show up for work is obviously serious. The job doesn't get done right or doesn't get done at all. The morale and productivity of other employees who depend on this person suffer because they can't operate as efficiently—especially if they have to work with a less skilled or inexperienced substitute when a regular employee is absent. If other employees see that the company tolerates shoddy performance or excessive absenteeism, they may think they can get by with less effort or that they can miss work with impunity.

The consequences for the fired employee are serious too. He or she loses an income and benefits that may be needed to support a family. A person who is fired for any cause most likely will feel rejected as a person, and his or her sense of self-worth may be diminished significantly. It may be difficult for this person to find another job at the same wage and benefit levels if future employers learn that he or she was fired "for cause."

How would a utilitarian approach some of the other situations discussed earlier like promising long-term employment and pension benefits to employees and then firing them or forcing them into early retirement because they can be replaced with younger people who wage and benefit packages won't cost as much? Again, the overall good and bad consequences both for the company and the employees would have to be weighed. Justice or respect for human persons would not, as such, be important. It's unlikely, however, that a company that treated employees this way would be able to attract good people over the long term or maintain a good public reputation needed to sell its product or services once the news of how it treated employees got around. That would be true as well for a company that fired employees whose unconventional behavior offended some people but didn't harm the business or who had blown the whistle or had refused sexual advances.

A company would also probably be obliged, even on utilitarian grounds, to give a person adequate warning that he or she might be fired for poor work or absenteeism. The exception would be where a person had done something dishonest or had deliberately done something that seriously harmed the company.

THE CULTURAL RELATIVIST'S APPROACH

Limits on a company's freedom to dismiss at will has to be determined, for the cultural relativist, purely and simply by society's laws and customs. In some cultures, employers might have complete control over who they fired and when and for what reasons. In others, laws and customs might restrict what could be considered "just cause" for dismissal. As we noted earlier, employment at will was the custom in the United States for many years. Employers often hired, promoted, and fired people purely on the basis of their gender, race, religious preferences, or disabled status. But legislation since the mid-sixties has restricted the absolute freedom to hire and fire.

SUMMARY

What moral rights do people have to their jobs? May they be fired for reasons that are not connected with their job performance? Is "employment at will" a morally justifiable practice?

The Natural-Law Approach

The natural-law moralist, guided by the concepts of justice and respect for persons, would support several key principles covering dismissal of employees.

No employer is morally obliged to keep someone on the payroll if his or her service is no longer needed; that would be unfair to the stockholders. Good managers will, of course, want to retrain productive and loyal employees whose jobs become obsolete and transfer them to other available jobs in the company if that's possible.

Employees who are performing at a fully satisfactory level have a right, in virtue of their human dignity, to keep their jobs and not be removed for reasons unrelated to performance or to the company's need for those positions in the operation of the business.

Companies should not encourage long-term employment by promising people raises, pension benefits, and recognition tied to long service and then terminating them just before they are eligible for pensions or because new people could be hired to do their jobs for lower pay.

Employees can and should be demoted or fired for incompetence, excessive absenteeism, and substance abuse when efforts to coach or rehabilitate them are not successful. People who commit illegal acts in the context of their jobs should be demoted or fired unless their supervisors condoned what was done.

Anyone whose job is in jeopardy for poor performance or absenteeism has a right to be warned well in advance that he or she may be demoted or fired.

The Utilitarian Approach

The utilitarian moralist will look at a company's dismissal practices in terms of their overall good and bad consequences for the business and its employees.

Unproductive, chronically absent, or substance-abusing employees harm a company's operations in serious ways because the job doesn't get done properly or doesn't get done at all. If a company tolerates inefficient performance or excessive absenteeism, other employees may be tempted to slack off or start missing a lot of work.

The consequences for an employee who is fired are certainly serious: he or she and his or her dependents lose their income and benefits. The employee's sense of self-worth is diminished and prospects for his or her future employment are threatened.

It's likely that the utilitarian calculus almost always will come down in favor of the company whenever job performance, chronic absence, and substance abuse are at issue.

Practices like dismissing long-term employees to avoid paying pensions or to save money by replacing them with newer, less expensive employees have to be judged in light of overall consequences for all concerned. When a company resorts to these practices on any regular kind of basis and they become known to the general public, that company will probably not be able to attract good employees in the future or maintain the good public reputation needed to market its products or services. The same conclusion would likely apply where people are fired for erratic but harmless behavior some manager doesn't like, for blowing the whistle, for refusing sexual advances, or when people are fired without advance notice.

The Cultural Relativist's Approach

The cultural relativist will simply abide by whatever a society's customary practices are, with respect to firing people, or what laws govern them. In the United States, for many years, employers were free to hire, demote, and fire people on the basis of gender, race, religion, or disabled status at their own whim, but recent legislation at all levels of government has considerably restricted that absolute freedom.

NOTE

1. Berg, Eric N. "U.S. Is Said to Pursue Pension Case," *The New York Times,* January 10, 1991, p. D7. Copyright © 1991 by The New York Times. Reprinted by permission.

10

Loyalty to a Company

WHAT LOYALTY MEANS

Loyalty is a prized virtue, at least as far as employers are concerned. Once a person accepts a job with a company, he or she is considered to owe it loyalty, both while employed and, under certain conditions, even after leaving the company.

Is loyalty to one's employer a moral obligation? It depends on just what loyalty is taken to mean.

If it means that people are expected to do their jobs at some acceptable level of competence or to do what their supervisors tell them to do, whether in terms of their job descriptions or day-to-day directives, then loyalty is a matter of moral obligation because these expectations are of the very essence of the employment contract.

Further, doing one's job includes the understanding (verified, more and more these days, in a formal document signed by the employee) that the employee will keep information like trade secrets, marketing plans, strategic decisions, and personnel information confidential and will not make their specifics, at least, the topic of conversation with outsiders, whether personal friends or the public media. This kind of information belongs to the company, and the company has all the proprietary rights that go along with ownership.

Any manager who violates these terms of the employment contract is subject to disciplinary action by the company, "up to and including dismissal" as official company documents frequently caution. A manager who discloses proprietary information to outsiders may even face a lawsuit by the company for damages. Clearly, loyalty in this sense involves a moral obligation.

Disputes about the meaning of loyalty arise when companies attempt to extend its scope beyond its legitimate sense. Employers may not ask managers, in the name of loyalty, to commit any actions considered flagrantly immoral (by the natural-law moralist, at least), for example, theft, direct harm to people or property—like dumping toxic wastes into a community's water supply, deceitful advertising practices, sexual or psychological harassment of employees, and illegitimate firing or demotion of an employee for non-job-related reasons—like refusal of sexual advances, or because of a lifestyle that has no bearing on job performance but offends the personal sensibilities of someone in higher management.

Since employers may not suborn any of these actions, it follows that managers may not carry them out under orders, at least not in any way that could be judged formal cooperation in an action of this kind.

Managers may not carry on activities that conflict with their companies' interests, unless the companies permit them for some good reason or other. Accountants, for example, should not solicit private clients who could legitimately be served by the accountant's own employer. Managers should not provide off-hours consulting services to competitors, nor attempt to patent inventions or sell technical processes they may have developed largely from information derived directly from their employment or by using company materials and facilities.

Are these restrictions limited? May companies compel managers to sign agreements that appear to be all-inclusive in restricting the outside activities in which they may engage? I doubt that companies have a right to insist on such sweeping limitations. It seems perfectly acceptable to me for an accountant, management specialist, engineer, or personnel specialist to offer his or her professional expertise to people or organizations who are not competitors or potential clients of his or her company. An accountant, for example, could help the elderly or disadvantaged prepare their income tax returns. A management specialist could consult with a small business that does not have any dealings with or doesn't compete with his or her company.

It is generally accepted as well that while certain techniques or documents or trade secrets and marketing plans are legitimately proprietary to a company, general managerial or other skills are not. For example, a manager who hones his or her organizing and planning skills, while working for one company is not morally restricted from leaving the company and using those skills on behalf of a new employer. Just because a company has provided a manager with training courses designed to enhance his or her management skills does not mean that this manager cannot use the general skills derived from that training in some other job with some other company.

I do believe that a manager who accepted a job with a company with the intention of getting some up-front managerial or special skill training and then left that company for a better-paying job or setting up his or her own private operation soon after the training is completed acted immorally. While no company expects that every new employee it trains will necessarily remain on the payroll for an extended period of time, it does have the right to expect that a person who has taken a position with it is acting in good faith and intends to use that training on the company's behalf, at least for some reasonable interval.

WHISTLE BLOWING

A "whistle blower" in the business world is one who accuses fellow employees or supervisors or company officers of illegal or immoral actions. Whistle blowing is internal if the accusation is made through the lines of supervision or other designated channels and external if it is reported to people or agencies outside the company, like civil authorities or the media. Consider two examples:

- A manager of an ink manufacturing plant said he asked his supervisors why detergents used to clean ink tubs were dumped behind the plant when there had to be a better, safer way of disposing of them. He said the company told him that there was no problem with dumping the materials on plant property because they were biodegradable. He decided to report the detergent dumping to the State Department of Environmental Conservation. Officials of that organization found that the detergents were not biodegradable and were in fact alkaline. The local county health director, however, claimed that the practice had not led to health hazards.[1]

- Two Ashland Oil executives "told Federal investigators that Ashland Oil had paid bribes to Middle Eastern government officials to obtain crude supplies . . . " ("They Whistled," 1988). Both were subsequently fired and later won settlements from the company for unlawful dismissal (Schiller, 1988).

The most likely justification for blowing the whistle is in situations where somebody in a company is engaging in or tolerating an activity that will harm employees, stockholders, or the public, and the only way to stop the activity is to inform the appropriate supervisors in the company or, if that channel seems blocked, civil authorities or the media.

Despite that apparently laudable justification for whistle blowing, it does not appear to be accepted by all business leaders. James M. Roche, for example, a former chairman of General Motors, believed that whistle blowing was just one more tactic designed to generate conflict and disharmony in business (Roche, 1971). His opinion seems to be widely shared, because people who engage in whistle blowing often suffer severe hardship.[2]

When is whistle blowing morally justified? Is it ever morally obligatory? Since the answers to these questions may vary depending on whether the whistle blowing is internal or external, I'll treat each variety separately.

INTERNAL WHISTLE BLOWING

Suppose a manager has good reason to suspect that another manager he or she doesn't supervise is falsifying expense accounts, or taking kickbacks from suppliers, or using company resources or equipment for personal projects, or stealing supplies and materials from the company, or moonlighting for a competitor. He or she may consider it a mark of loyalty to the company to blow the whistle on a fellow employee who is stealing from or otherwise harming it. Is it permissible to blow the whistle on this person?

The answer is "certainly," provided some basic cautions are observed.

- It should be evident that the harm to the company is significant. Incidental taking of inexpensive office supplies, while wrong, may not be worth the effort or the harm done to an employee who is an asset to the company in other respects.

- The whistle blower has to be sure of his or her facts. A mistaken accusation may seriously damage another's reputation, even if it turns out that the allegation was false.

- The whistle blower should probably try to find out whether the suspect's activity is already known to supervision, perhaps as a result of audits or discreet investigations by company security.

- There should be some reasonable expectation that blowing the whistle will be effective, that the suspect's supervisors will put a stop to what is going on because they believe that the offense is as serious as the whistle blower thinks it is.

- The whistle blower has to consider the possible damage to his or her own reputation and prospects in the business. Will the action be seen as loyalty or simply as petty tattling, or an act of spite, or a chance to smear a rival for promotion? Will the whistle blower be labeled a troublemaker, however good his or her intentions?

- Finally, the manager might find out that in some instances, like using company equipment for personal use, simply confronting the guilty employee with his or her wrongdoing might be enough to stop it.

Is it morally obligatory to blow the whistle on a fellow manager? The answer to this question begins with establishing who has the primary obligation to watch out for and investigate any questionable action by any employee.

If a manager were to sign an agreement with the company acknowledging a responsibility to report, through the proper lines of supervision, all instances of possible wrongdoing he or she might encounter, there would of course be a moral obligation to blow the whistle whenever that was the case. But such explicit, formal agreements are probably very rare.

A manager's immediate supervisor is the first line of defense against dishonesty. Every supervisor needs to be satisfied that expense vouchers of all kinds submitted by subordinates are reasonable and reflect only costs incurred for legitimate company business. Any action that smacks of dishonesty or of misuse of company property or materials has to be dealt with as soon as the supervisor becomes aware of it. This is part of a supervisor's job description and a part of the promise to do the job he or she is being paid to do. As such, it is a matter of moral obligation. The same is true of all levels of supervision up through the chain of command.

Another defense against employee dishonesty is the security organization, where it exists in a company. Its responsibility is to help protect company assets. It must, for instance, take steps to insure that materials, supplies, and equipment are not illicitly removed from company premises. To this end, it might initiate random inspection of briefcases and handbags. Or it may require that anyone carrying a piece of equipment out of a building show a clearance pass or tag before leaving with it.

Auditing staffs have the responsibility of reviewing all aspects of expense accounts, purchasing contracts, and adherence to company financial reporting procedures, and have an obligation by virtue of the job they are paid to do to report any irregularities or violations to appropriate levels of management.

I believe that a manager who finds out that a fellow employee not under his or her supervision is stealing from or otherwise harming the company may assume that the safeguards just described are operating and that they may be relied upon to catch the wrongdoer. Consequently, I see no strict moral obligation to blow the whistle on this person, unless the manager is sure that these safeguards are not working and there is a question of very serious harm to the company. This obligation would arise where a manager by virtue of his or her special assignment or unique expertise in some area would be the only person competent to spot certain kinds of wrongdoing and was reasonably certain that it was not readily apparent to supervisors, auditors, or the security organization. It's probable, however, that such situations are rare.

EXTERNAL WHISTLE BLOWING

A manager who reports company wrongdoing to civil authorities or the media is engaging in external whistle blowing. When is this action permissible? Is it ever obligatory?

In addition to the cautions listed earlier for the internal whistle blower, several others seem to be required before external whistle blowing is justified.

- An effort has to be made to report wrongful conduct internally, through proper lines of organization. The company should have a chance to clean up its act before the whistle blower goes public. It should be evident that higher management, up through the board of directors, refused to take the steps necessary to stop the wrongdoing.
- It must be evident that external agencies like outside auditors or public regulatory bodies are unable or unwilling to report what is going on.
- A significant case of harm to stockholders, employees, or the public has to be at issue such as fraud or embezzlement, unsafe working conditions, or dumping of hazardous materials in areas that will harm people and the environment.
- The degree of harm that the company will suffer as a result of the

whistle blowing should be proportionate to the harm its wrongdoing is causing.

Given that all these conditions were satisfied, it would certainly be permissible for a manager to blow the whistle to outsiders.

When would external whistle blowing be morally obligatory?

The primary obligation for preventing and stopping wrongdoing lies with supervision. The more responsibility a manager has for company operations, the stronger that obligation is. I believe that a manager would be obliged to report wrongdoing to outsiders only if serious harm were at issue and it was evident that appropriate levels of supervision were unwilling to stop it, or other managers knowing about it refused to report it, or any external agencies that could stop it had no way of knowing it was going on. Again, this obligation is more evident when for some reason, by virtue of his or her unique position in the company or special expertise, a manager would be the only person who would know enough about the situation to report it creditably.

The conclusions I have drawn about obligatory internal whistle blowing would be supported by the natural-law moralist on the grounds of justice, that is, whenever a person's direct managerial responsibilities to the company would require that he or she take steps to make misconduct known. I think this moralist would support optional internal whistle blowing and external whistle blowing on the principle that unjustified harm to others should be prevented.

A utilitarian moralist would need to examine the good and bad consequences for everyone involved in the situation that would result from either internal or external whistle blowing.

The cultural relativist would probably rely heavily on what society thinks about whistle blowing. In the United States, for instance, government employees who blow the whistle are protected by law against retaliation. The government appears to think that whistle blowers are demonstrating a high degree of loyalty when they report wrongdoing. In the private sector, however, whistle blowers seem to be regarded as little better than "informers," so there is a good possibility that our culture would not require any variety of blowing the whistle where private business is concerned.

COMMENTS ON THE CASES

Let's look now at the two cases of whistle blowing I described earlier, one where a manager reported his former company for dumping toxic material behind its plant and the other that involved two vice presidents of an oil company who told federal investigators that their company had made payments to Mid-Eastern government officials. What might be said about these cases in light of the moral guidelines just proposed on whistle blowing?

The plant manager who reported dumping of toxic wastes said he had talked to his management about it but the company had refused to stop the practice. His next recourse was to blow the whistle externally, to a state government agency.

Was that action morally permissible? If the manager had good reason to suspect that serious harm was being done and assuming that the company refused to do anything about it, it probably was. He may have even felt that he had a moral obligation to report the dumping. As it turned out, a county health official claimed the dumping was not a threat to the public. If that was true and the whistle blower knew it (in this case, he apparently didn't) the action would certainly not be morally obligatory, and, in view of the potential harm to the company, probably not even permissible.

What about the two vice presidents of an oil company who told federal investigators about their company's payments to foreign officials? Both, it appears, had attempted to deal with these payments through appropriate company channels. One of them had told the company's chairman that they were probably illegal and later sent material describing them to each member of the board of directors (Schiller).

Was internal whistle blowing justified? It looks like the vice president who told the chairman and the board of directors about the payments certainly did the right thing because of the potential harm that would be done to the company if it were found guilty of making them. In effect, it was certainly morally permissible, in my judgment. Was it obligatory? Probably not, if higher-level, more responsible executives knew about it.

Should they have gone external, for instance, to the government, on their own? Without knowing a lot more facts, it's only possible to speculate. To justify a direct disclosure to the government without the pressure of official outside investigators the damage that the bribery caused would have to have been weighed against the harm done to the company by its disclosure. The payments' effect on competitors who may have bid honestly for the crude oil and might have won the contract for it would have to weigh heavily in this assessment along with the interests of the citizens of the country whose officials accepted the payments and may have failed to get the best price for the crude. The issue of contributing to the moral turpitude of the people who took the payments would have to be factored in as well.

THE MORALITY OF FIRING WHISTLE BLOWERS

Are companies ever justified in firing, demoting, or cutting short the careers of whistle blowers? I don't think there are any legitimate grounds whatever to discipline whistle blowers in any way as long as they have reported a genuine case of misconduct and attempted to do it through appropriate channels or have gone outside the company only as a last resort. A company would be justified in taking action against an employee who deliberately lied about a case, or knowingly misrepresented it so that it looked more serious than it really was, or had clearly blown the whistle just as an act of revenge on a fellow employee or supervisor or to protest a company policy he or she didn't like, or was attempting to discredit a rival for promotion. But a whistle blower, whether internal or external, who has uncovered a legitimate case of wrongdoing that was not discovered and treated through the ordinary supervisory and security procedures or was simply ignored by responsible levels of supervision has performed a morally praiseworthy act, if he or she has stepped in to prevent or stop a serious harm to people or the environment, a harm that could not be justified by company officials. Therefore, it would be a clear case of injustice, a patently immoral act, to punish that person for doing what was morally right, just to get revenge on him or her or to appease higher levels of management who might not like "tattle-tales."

Nor does a claim of self-defense justify punitive action against whistle blowers, that is, the claim that the person has caused trouble for the company and might do it again. Unjust aggression alone justifies self-defense, and legitimate whistle blowers are not unjust aggressors.

WHAT LOYALTY DOESN'T MEAN

Sometimes managers believe that loyalty to the boss means covering up for his or her serious mistakes or, even wrongdoing. That belief is simply false, in my opinion. A manager has a fiduciary duty to the owners of the business, and it would be a violation of that duty to cover up actions by a supervisor that were harming the owners' interests in any serious way.

A subordinate has to carry out the legitimate orders of his or her supervisor and keep him or her informed about how things are going in an assignment. He or she may even be obliged to tell the boss about actions of other persons or groups that may adversely affect the boss's operations. But wrongdoing by a boss may not be ignored. If a subordinate thinks his or her boss is doing something wrong, the subordinate's first option is to confront the boss with the situation. If that doesn't appear to work, the subordinate may have to go to higher management. I believe that the guidelines for whistle blowing would be helpful in deciding how to proceed here.

SUMMARY

Employers value and expect loyalty from their employees. Is loyalty to a company a moral obligation?

When loyalty to a firm means requiring managers to do their jobs competently, to obey the legitimate orders of supervisors, keep proprietary information and trade secrets confidential, and avoid conduct that conflicts with a company's rightful interests, managers do have a moral obligation to be loyal. But employers may not ask managers to show their loyalty by committing illegal or immoral actions like dumping toxic wastes near a community's water supply, engaging in deceitful advertising, or harassing, demoting, or even firing employees for nonjob-related reasons—like refusing sexual advances. Managers, in turn, may not use loyalty as a rationale for formally cooperating in morally wrong actions their supervisors may ask them to perform.

A manager who learns and practices managerial or other skills in a company, skills that become part of his or her "person," is not disloyal if he or she decides to leave and use those skills somewhere else. It would be morally wrong, however, for a manager to join a company just to get certain managerial or technical training knowing full well that he or she did not intend to work for that company for some reasonable period.

Whistle blowing, accusing fellow employees, supervisors, or company officers of illegal or immoral actions either through company channels or to agencies outside the company, looks like a prime example of disloyal behavior. When is it morally justified? To answer that question adequately, the two varieties of whistle blowing, internal and external, have to be analyzed separately.

Blowing the whistle internally on a fellow employee seems permissible when:

- the harm being done to the company is significant;
- the whistle blower is sure of his or her facts;

- it is likely that the offending party's supervisors do not know what is going on;
- there is a reasonable expectation that blowing the whistle will be effective;
- the whistle blower's reputation and prospects in the business won't be seriously harmed;
- directly confronting the wrongdoer will not make him or her stop what he or she is doing.

The obligation to blow the whistle internally seems to depend on who has the primary responsibility for discovering and investigating an employee's questionable actions. An employee's immediate supervisor, has to be alert for any seriously questionable actions a subordinate might perform like making up false expense vouchers or misusing company funds, property, or materials. A company's security organization, if it has one, is responsible for helping protect company assets. Auditing staffs need to review expense accounts, purchasing contracts, and adherence to company financial reporting procedures. I believe that a manager is morally *obliged* to blow the whistle internally when he or she holds one of these positions of responsibility and discovers wrongdoing, or, if not in one of these positions, is sure that the ordinary safeguards against defrauding the company or misusing its assets are not working, or when he or she has some unique expertise in virtue of which only he or she can understand and identify the wrongdoing.

A decision to blow the whistle externally, to some outside party, seems allowed when all the conditions for internal whistle blowing have been satisfied and:

- an effort has been made to report wrongful conduct internally, through the proper lines of organization, so that the company has a chance to clean up its act before the whistle blower goes public;
- external agencies like outside auditors or public regulatory bodies can't or won't take appropriate action;
- a significant harm to the company, its employees, or the public is at issue;
- the harm the company will suffer from the whistle blowing is proportional to the harm it is causing by its wrongdoing.

A manager would be obliged to blow the whistle externally, in my opinion, only if company supervision knew about and refused to take action in a situation where the interests of shareholders, employees, or the public were being seriously harmed or threatened and no other responsible person in the company would speak out. Again, possessing certain special expertise in the matter at issue would strengthen a manager's obligation.

The natural-law moralist would support these conclusions I have drawn about whistle blowing on the grounds of justice, what one owes to one's company, or on the grounds that we ought to prevent unjustified harm to others. The utilitarian moralist would want to weigh all the good and bad consequences that would result from an act of either internal or external whistle blowing. The cultural relativist would want to determine what laws might be at issue. There are, for example, laws protecting government employees from retaliation for blowing the whistle. In private industry, however, whistle blowers are often looked on as "informers," so there is at least some question as to whether our culture would ever require blowing the whistle on private business.

We looked at two cases of whistle blowing, one where a manager reported his company externally for dumping toxic material behind its plant, and one involving two vice presidents of an oil company who were fired because they told federal investigators that their company had made payments to Mid-Eastern government officials in order to secure a source of crude oil. Both had reported the matter internally.

The action of the plant manager was permissible as long as he thought real harm was being done or could be done. Since a county health official thought no harm was in fact being done, the external whistle blowing was not obligatory, and, if the manager knew that before he went external (in this case, he apparently didn't), possibly not even permissible in view of the potential damage that action would cause the company.

In the second case, the vice presidents did the right thing by informing top management of the illegal payments, by blowing the whistle internally. They knew the serious damage that the company's reputation would suffer if the payments become public. To blow the whistle externally, however, would have required them to weigh the harm to the company against the effects the payments had on competitors and on the citizens in the Mid-Eastern country whose interests may have been damaged if the right price was not paid for their oil. The characters of the officials who took the payments were affected, and that would have to figure into the decision.

I concluded that there is no moral justification for firing whistle blowers who uncover cases of wrongdoing that involve serious harm to people or the environment and couldn't have been stopped any other way, through the usual company channels. To do so would be to unjustly punish someone for doing what was morally right.

Finally, we looked at the idea that loyalty is sometimes taken to mean covering up for a supervisor's errors or wrongdoing. That is a false belief, because managers have a fiduciary responsibility to the stockholders, and that duty would be violated if a supervisor's wrongdoing that was harming the owners' interests went unreported.

Subordinates do have to carry out the legitimate orders of their supervisors and keep them informed about the status of the operations for which they are responsible. If a subordinate thinks his or her boss is doing something wrong, the first step is to confront the boss with the situation. If that doesn't resolve the issue, higher management may have to be told about it. The guidelines for blowing the whistle might be useful in deciding what to do in these kinds of cases.

NOTES

1. Snel, A. "A Manager Who Blew the Whistle," *The Progressive*, April 1985, p. 17. Reprinted by permission from *The Progressive*, 409 East Main Street, Madison, Wisconsin 53703.

2. For some illustrative accounts of what happens to whistle blowers, see the April, 1985 issue of *Good Housekeeping* or the June 23, 1986 issue of *New York*.

11

Employee and Public Safety

SAFETY AT WORK

A few years ago, it was reported that

> The Peabody Coal Company has pleaded guilty to felony charges of violating Federal mine safety regulations stemming from the death of a worker. . . . Peabody acknowledged it allowed miners to work under an unsupported roof at its Eagle Mine No. 2 near Shawneetown, the prosecutor said. . . . One miner was killed when the roof fell.[1]

The thousands of accidents where workers have been killed or seriously injured help explain why Congress passed the Occupational and Safety Health Act (OSHA). The lawmakers simply could not ignore the high incidence of work-related deaths and injuries in the American workplace, many or perhaps most of which might have been prevented by providing effective safety procedures and devices and by eliminating potential hazards to workers. While employers frequently complain about the stringency of OSHA rules or argue that many of them are trite or inapplicable in given work situations, they nevertheless carry a clear legal obligation to provide a safe and healthy work environment.

Since the health and physical integrity of human beings is at stake where they work, there is a moral as well as legal obligation to take all reasonable steps to insure that they are safe there. How far does this moral duty extend? What does it require of managers?

It's important to distinguish the moral problems raised by allowing people to work in unsafe physical and, perhaps, psychological surroundings from those created by work that is considered hazardous in itself such as handling radioactive materials, performing daredevil stunts, riveting structural beams on skyscrapers, or treating people with highly infectious diseases. The concern here is with the moral obligation employers have, for example, to ventilate mine shafts or areas where hazardous gases or chemicals are present; insure that buildings are structurally sound; furnish protective garments and goggles and power equipment screens and shields; keep hand and power tools in good operating condition; provide accurate radiation counters for people who work with radioactive materials; bolt heavy filing cabinets and shelving to the wall; and provide employee safety training and safety awareness programs.

The strongest argument for not providing or only providing minimally safe working conditions is, of course, cost. Safety is expensive and reduces earnings available for reinvestment in the business or for paying dividends to stockholders.

THE UTILITARIAN APPROACH

The correct utilitarian answer in cases involving safety on the job requires weighing the cost of providing safety measures against the probability of serious harm or death to human beings, the financial losses that injured employees and their families would suffer, the emotional distress inflicted on those families, and the potential cost of lawsuits and settlements if the company were found liable for an industrial accident. If the cost of taking safety measures were conceivably high enough to force a company out of existence, the impact that would have on its employees and owners and the communities supported by its operations would have to be considered as well. I believe that if the probability of harm to human life and limb were high, that consideration would have to carry a lot of weight in the utilitarian's calculation. The difficulty here is to set a value on human life and physical integrity that is commensurate with the economic values at stake.

THE NATURAL–LAW APPROACH

For the natural-law moralist, the major concern would be the probability and immediacy of serious harm to a human being. The basic principle at work here is that no one may put his or her person in serious jeopardy, either continuously or on a sometime basis, without an extremely compelling reason. Making a living just doesn't seem to meet that test. It may seem callous, of course, to claim that a person who is caught up in harsh economic circumstances and is working in unsafe surroundings is morally obliged to quit and find another job, but that seems to be the only conclusion a natural-law moralist could reach. An individual might tolerate working for a short time in unsafe conditions while they were in the process of being corrected, or while he or she was looking for another job or finishing out time to reach entitlement to some benefit like a pension, but there would have to be a limit on how long that could go on, depending on the seriousness and immediacy of the threat.

Suppose that limited skills or knowledge hindered a person from finding another job with equivalent levels of pay and benefits. A decision to quit might have serious financial implications for his or her family. Would that situation satisfy a natural-law moralist as justification for continuing to work in an unsafe environment? Probably not. For one thing, it would be a short-sighted decision which failed to consider what would happen to the individual's family in the long run if he or she were seriously injured or killed at work. A company that can't provide safe working conditions probably can't or is unwilling to provide any significant amount of benefits to a worker's beneficiaries. But most importantly, the economic effects by themselves would not be enough to allow a person to put himself or herself in serious danger, no matter how freely that decision was made. There are other alternatives for supporting a family, even if they don't provide the exact same life-style the family may have grown accustomed to. And individuals usually have opportunities to upgrade their skills and knowledge which will prepare them for better jobs.

What if employees were willing, because of economic hardship, to work where they were unsafe? Would that get employers off the hook? The natural-law moralist would have to answer "no" on a couple of counts. If an individual may not put himself or herself in serious jeopardy without good reason, it would be immoral for anyone else to cooperate in that act. Further, it would be morally unconscionable for a company to take advantage of its employees' financial distress for its own economic gain. The utilitarian moralist, I think, would come to the same conclusion after considering all the consequences, with the value of life and limb probably carrying no small weight in the calculation.

THE CULTURAL RELATIVIST'S APPROACH

In order to make a moral judgment about a company's responsibility for safety, a cultural relativist would need to know what laws governed safety practices in the workplace. In the United States, for instance, the Occupational Safety and Health Act (OSHA) passed by Congress in 1970 has made employers responsible for eliminating existing and potential hazards to employees from the working environment. If no specific laws applied, then whatever practices society tolerated would have to count. Some societies might think that owners and managers alone should decide how much they are willing to invest in safe working conditions. It would be up to the workers, then, to decide whether or not to work where they might be exposed to serious physical hazards. That freedom could, of course, be restricted if a particular industry having little regard for safety were the only place where a person could get a decent job. In that case, workers would have to put up with unsafe working conditions. The question then arises whether the cultural relativist would be willing to equate that toleration to "custom," so that the employer would be morally blameless if employees were injured or killed on the job.

Where unions bargain for safe work practices and a safe work environment, it probably would be "customary," in the absence of specific laws, for employers to abide by these agreements with unions, and those agreements, sanctioned directly or indirectly by society, would constitute the moral standard against which safe working conditions would have to be measured.

The Coal Company Case

In a case like that of the coal company reported earlier, the natural-law moralist would have to conclude that the managers involved were clearly morally responsible for the death of their employee if they were fully aware that serious unsafe conditions were present in their mine and intentionally refused to correct them. Further, the company and its managers would be liable, morally, to make restitution for the financial damage suffered by the employee who was killed and his family. They would also be morally liable for the emotional suffering of the family and might be required to compensate its members for that suffering to the extent it could be measured in dollars and cents.

The fact that correcting the unsafe conditions might drive a company out of business would not be an acceptable defense for these moralists, nor, I suspect, for utilitarians once they weighed all the consequences involved. If companies cannot afford reasonable corrections to physical or psychological working conditions that carry a high probability of causing death or serious injury, they should not continue to operate, no matter what the cost to the communities they operate in, to the shareholders, and to employees—none of whose economic rights can ever outweigh the right of human beings to work in a reasonably safe place. (Remember, I'm not talking about high-risk *occupations* but about high-risk, correctable conditions incidental to the tasks themselves. Mining coal is a high-risk occupation, but steps can be taken to reduce its risks.)

Cultural relativists would look to laws or accepted customs in deciding what the coal company was obliged to do to protect their employees.

PUBLIC SAFETY

The case of the Ford Motor Company's Pinto has been widely publicized. The alleged scenario is that the Company wanted to produce a low-priced, sporty car to compete with similar models marketed by foreign car makers. In order to hold down the model's cost and price it competitively, every effort was made to keep it lightweight and maximize its gas mileage. Tests of the model indicated that in the event of a rear-end collision above a certain speed, its gas tank was likely to rupture, spill gasoline, and catch fire. The Company's engineers experimented with modifications that would eliminate the problem with the tank but would add about $11 or so to the cost of every vehicle. The Company did a cost-benefit study that set the value of a human life at around $200,000 and concluded that the cost of changing over to a safer gas tank was significantly greater than the cost of all the human lives that might be lost in accidents involving these vehicles. The Company decided not to change the tank's design.

In the late 1970's, hundreds of families had to abandon their homes permanently when it was learned that fumes from toxic wastes stored by a chemical company years before at a nearby dump site had contaminated them. Here's part of the story behind that disaster:

> The Hooker Chemicals and Plastics Corporation knew as early as 1958 that toxic industrial chemicals that it had dumped into the Love Canal site at

Niagara Falls years before were seeping into surrounding areas containing private homes, a school and playground, according to documents made public today by the House subcommittee on oversight and investigations. . . . Hooker officials testified that they had warned the owners of the dump site through informal discussions, but had not taken steps to publicize the existence of the chemicals or to warn nearby residents, because the company did not feel it was responsible for doing so.[2]

A myriad of cases could be cited where the safety of the public or customers has been jeopardized by companies, but the two just described sufficiently illustrate the fact that the bottom line is apparently too frequently the sole criterion some managers use in deciding how safe to make their products or how closely they should control manufacturing and processing operations.

Most of us, I think, would agree that the world cannot be made absolutely safe. Human beings make mistakes that result in unintended harm to others. Materials used in manufacturing follow natural physical laws: metals, for instance may bend or break from some structural weakness not predictable in manufacturing or design processes; the most carefully designed containers may fail and allow toxic chemicals to leak from them. We are aware that the use of many human artifacts entails some risk.

However, where it is known that the design of a product or the process used to make it poses a serious threat to human life or limb, is the manufacturer required to eliminate the hazard or tell the public about it so that we can decide whether we want to chance using it or prevent it from being made?

The Dangerous Gas Tank

Let's first examine the issue of selling a product with a known design flaw that makes it potentially dangerous to its users. Since I cited a case involving an automobile, I'll use that as the illustrative instance for our moral analysis.

I think that it's reasonable to assume that a person's ordinary knowledge and experience can be relied on to make him or her aware of the features of a product that might make it unsafe in certain circumstances. In the case of automobiles, for instance, nobody expects them to be made absolutely safe, at least not given our present state of technology, and everyone understands that it is possible to be seriously injured or killed in a car crash. It's pretty obvious that a small, light car will not withstand a collision as well as a larger, heavier one, but a person might choose to take a risk and buy the small car anyway because it is cheaper to own and operate. A car equipped with air bags is surely safer than one that isn't, but a customer might still elect to buy the less expensive model. The point here is that the buyer has the ability in these instances to estimate the probability of being involved in an accident that might result in serious harm or even death and decide whether the risk warrants spending more money on a safer car or saving money on a less safe model. It seems to me that there is no moral requirement for automobile manufacturers to point out these facts to all potential customers; they may reasonably assume that prospective buyers are aware of them.

But people do have some basic expectations about the reliability of cars they purchase and the obligation of the manufacturers to meet them. They assume that any known design flaw will not jeopardize their safety. Everyone, while fully recognizing that the unpredictable can happen, that an unforeseen flaw can cause a mechanical failure, nevertheless expects brakes and lights to work, steering components to hang together, wheels to stay on, electrical and fuel systems not to catch fire in an accident (unless the kind of accident involved would be so violent as to cause any automobile to burn), and expects that the vehicle will not tip over when making sharp turns at reasonable speeds. Automobile manufacturers do have a moral obligation out of the respect owed human beings to honor these expectations, to tell potential customers anything about the design of their vehicles that could seriously jeopardize the safety of those riding in them, any flaws that people could not be expected to identify just from their own everyday knowledge and experience.

Someone might argue that the principle of double effect used by some natural-law moralists would justify a car manufacturer's decision not to tell the public about potentially dangerous design flaws in a particular model. The justification would go something like this: first, the act of manufacturing an automobile for purposes of making a profit is morally all right in itself. Next, the manufacturer intends only the good effects, that is, furnishing a useful product to customers and providing economic benefits to shareholders, employees, and the community. Third, the evil effect of possible serious injury or death to a human being is only a foreseen but unintended consequence. So far so good. However, I believe that the final condition for successfully applying the double effect principle, that is, the required due proportion between the good and evil effects, is not satisfied. In the case we just talked about, the gas tank that was highly vulnerable to rupturing in a rear-end collision, I think it's important to remember that the likelihood of deaths due to the design itself was known beforehand, so it wasn't enough to say that everybody knows that any car might burn if hit from the rear; the point is that this model, simply by virtue of its design, was apparently far more vulnerable in rear-end collisions at a particular speed than others, and the manufacturer seemed to be fully aware of that fact. It's hard to see, then, how the usefulness of this product and the financial benefits selling it would generate for shareholders, employees and political communities would outweigh even the relatively few lives of the people who would be killed because of its flawed design.

The utilitarian moralist's calculus would come up with the same answer, I think, as the application of the double effect principle would.

The cultural relativist would have to consult laws or customs. If no laws applied, what practices society expected and tolerated from manufacturers would have to be respected.

As for the cost-benefit analysis used by the company in the case cited, I would conclude that the attempt to put a dollar value on human life before the fact of an accident does not wash, morally speaking. Attempts are made, of course, to estimate the dollar value of life and limb for purposes of settling lawsuits over incidents where injury or death have already occurred. It's hard though, to see how they can be reduced to just one more element to be considered in a future-oriented financial decision where profit and loss constitute the ultimate values against which everything else has to be weighed.

MAKING RISKS PUBLIC

Would going public with a product's unsafe design feature get a company off the moral hook? That would, of course, allow people to assess the risk of using it for themselves. Certain toys, for example, may be unsafe for toddlers but perfectly safe for older children. Where the risk of harm is very high, however, in the case of a toy that would be extremely dangerous for a child of any age to play with, the morally correct solution would be to keep the product off the market entirely. Simply telling prospective buyers about the danger would not be enough.

So it seems that a good rule for managers to follow here should be that if it is certain that making a product's unsafe design features known to the public would mean that it wouldn't sell, the morally correct action would be not to manufacture it. If some models of the product had already been manufactured, they would have to be kept off the market—even if that were to result in financial losses to the manufacturer.

The Leaching Toxic Waste

Assigning moral responsibility and liability for restitution in the case of the chemical company could be a little more complex. If the company knowingly ignored safe storage practices and was aware that the contamination and resultant damage was likely to occur, the conclusion is obvious: the responsible managers were guilty of committing a moral wrong which was further compounded by their failure to warn the public about the menace. They would also be morally liable to make restitution for all damage caused.

If, however, a company follows accepted standards ("B.A.T." or "Best Available Technology") in disposing of the waste and has no reason to suspect that leaching would occur, a different judgment seems called for. We are responsible for those consequences of our actions that we can reasonably be expected to foresee. If it were true that the people in the company who stored the waste did not have reason to suspect that it would leach, they could not be charged with knowingly and willingly causing harm and could not be held *morally* responsible for what happened. Would they be liable for making restitution for all damages? After all, it was *their* toxic waste that leached. It seems to follow, on the face of it, that if the company could not be charged with moral responsibility for what happened, it could not be held morally accountable for resulting damages.

But that leaves those people whose health and property were affected holding the bag. It surely seems like they should have some moral claim on the company. One way to press their claim would be to argue that the company, in knowingly and willingly undertaking a manufacturing process whose waste products could be hazardous to people and the environment if they were ever exposed to them, also had to at least implicitly assume responsibility even if the exposure was purely accidental. That would count as "reasonably foreseeing" the consequences of its actions, and the company would be morally accountable for them. It's like driving a car. The judgment of the general public seems to be that I must be assumed to "foresee" *any damage whatever* I may do to people or property while driving, and that I am, consequently, liable for it. That's why many states in the United States require drivers to carry liability insurance.

The problem with this kind of argument is that it seems to carry "foreseeing" too far. It is possible, of course, that every time I drive my car I might kill someone—even though I conscientiously follow safe driving practices. I might, for instance, make an honest misjudgment in speed or distance. But if I do not knowingly and willingly do something which results in harm to someone else's life, limb, or property, I cannot be held morally responsible for it. How, then, can I be morally liable for restitution for the harm I may have done? Is it that it is "unfair" for the person harmed to have to bear the brunt of accidental damage caused by someone else? It's hard to see how this unfairness could be attributed to the person causing the damage when he or she is assumed to be innocent of any malice. It's not unlike situations where "acts of God" or chance or fate are invoked as the cause of natural disasters affecting people and their property. We don't usually think of the result as being morally "unfair"; we do think it "bad luck" and tragic that someone has to suffer the physical and financial burdens that go along with it. That's why we take up collections for disaster relief or, more importantly, establish insurance to protect against the effects of potential disasters.

The natural-law moralist's approach to the issue of liability in this kind of situation is that one is not morally responsible for consequences he or she produces but did not intend or reasonably foresee. Nor is he or she required to make restitution for harm done, unless it is currently underway and can be stopped. In that case, the person is morally bound to stop it. There is, however, no liability for damages until he or she is aware that they are occurring (O'Connell, 1962). The chemical company in the case we have been examining would, on this account, be morally bound to intervene and try to stop the leaching and, certainly, be bound to warn people about the danger to their health and property. Notifying the new owners of the dump site was not enough; the leaching was a consequence of the chemical company's action, not the new owner's.

The utilitarian moralist would, of course, weigh all the good and bad consequences for everyone involved and decide whether or not the company was bound to warn people and take steps to stop the leaching once it knew about it or whether that responsibility really belonged to the new owner.

For the cultural relativist, whatever law dictated or custom tolerated would have to prevail.

SUMMARY

Cases abound where people are seriously injured or killed in the workplace. People are also killed by unsafe products. What moral obligations do managers have to provide safe working conditions for their employees and ensure that their products do not harm the public?

We examined cases where a miner was killed when a hazardous mine roof went unrepaired, where an automobile's gas tank was likely to explode and burn in a rear-end collision, and where toxic material leached from a dump site, poisoning the surrounding area and making it unfit for humans to live in. The concern expressed for worker safety was not with occupations that were hazardous by nature but with situations where managers tolerated unsafe, correctable conditions in the work environment.

Natural-law moralists would likely argue that it is morally wrong to put anyone at serious risk just because it would cost money and dilute profits to eliminate hazards. Nor would these moralists think it right for a person to subject himself or herself to these hazards on the grounds of economic necessity. That's also why managers responsible for hazardous working conditions would not get off the moral hook even if their employees were willing to work in unsafe surroundings.

The utilitarian moralist would have to project and weigh the good and bad consequences for shareholders, employees, and the community before deciding whether it would be morally right for managers to tolerate unsafe working conditions. The threat to human life and limb would have to weigh heavily in this comparison, assuming that their value could be meaningfully measured against the economic values at stake.

The cultural relativist would need to conform to any laws governing safety, or, in the absence of such laws, determine what society's customs required managers to do, if anything, about keeping workers safe. It might be "customary," for example, to let union-management bargaining agreements establish safe working conditions and practices that management would then be morally obliged to follow.

In the case where an unsafe mine roof fell in and killed a worker, the natural-law moralist would surely find the company's managers morally responsible for failure to correct seriously unsafe conditions if those managers were fully aware of the hazard and intentionally ignored it. I believe that the utilitarian moralist would come to the same conclusion.

The cultural relativist would look to laws or custom to determine whether or not the company was morally responsible for what happened.

As for product safety, I argued that no one can expect all products to be completely safe. When unpredictable human error or unknown and unforeseen weakness in materials cause harm, no moral blame may be laid at a manufacturer's doorstep. As we saw, however, in the case of the unsafe automobile gas tank, when a product's threat to life and limb can be predicted, and the threat is due to a weakness inherent in the product, a manufacturer, out of respect for persons, may not hide that fact.

I believe that both natural-law and (depending on the specifics of each case) utilitarian moralists would agree that if people know about a product's potential for injury and can take reasonable precautions against it, it would be morally correct to sell the item, but a highly risky product probably should be kept off the market entirely. The cultural relativist would rely on existing laws or customs to decide whether potentially harmful products should not be sold to the public.

In the case of leaching toxic waste, the natural-law and utilitarian moralists would be concerned with what consequences a company's managers could reasonably foresee. The natural-law moralist would likely require the company originally responsible for establishing the toxic waste dump site to clean it up once its managers were aware it was leaking. The utilitarian moralist would weigh the good and bad consequences that would result if the company responsible for the site were to refuse to clean it up. Finally, the cultural relativist would resort to whatever laws or customs governed this kind of situation.

NOTES

1. "Peabody Coal Co. Pleads Guilty in Miner's Death," *The New York Times*, June 4, 1986, p. A15. Copyright © 1986 by The New York Times Company. Reprinted by permission.

2. Weisman, S. R. "Hooker Company Knew About Toxic Peril in 1958," *The New York Times*, April 11, 1979, p. B1, B6. Copyright © 1979 by The New York Times Company. Reprinted by permission.

12

Truth in the Free–Market Economic System

THE FREE–ENTERPRISE SYSTEM

Apologists for the capitalist free-enterprise system argue that in its American version, at least, it has produced the highest standard of living for more people than any other system; no purely socialist economy, for instance, is likely to equal capitalism's power to generate such a broad variety of products or distribute wealth so widely in the societies in which it operates. The reasons for this are as follows:

- There is complete freedom to enter the market as buyer or seller. Anyone may elect to offer a product or service to buyers; buyers are free to purchase or not purchase it.
- Buyers and sellers are free to exchange goods and services at mutually satisfactory prices.
- Scarce resources are allocated efficiently because only those goods and services will be produced that people want to buy.
- A wide variety of products are made available to the buying public.
- Those people who are willing to work harder and more efficiently and are able to design, package, and market more attractive products will be rewarded financially while those who can't will not survive. High-priced, poor quality products and services will not make it in the marketplace.

- Competition is the key to the free-enterprise system. Because sellers of goods and services have to vie with each other for the customer's dollar, they will offer high-quality wares at the lowest possible prices. All the participants in the arena need is a level playing ground: no competitor should have an edge or advantage not justified within the system if the system is to yield the best results.

- All members of the society in which the free market operates will prosper directly or indirectly (for example, through social welfare programs of various kinds) from the wealth generated by the market.

That, at least, is the *theory* of the free market system to which everyone engaged in it claims to be committed. But how does the market really operate in the United States? Why do our news media almost routinely include accounts of actual and alleged ethical misconduct by corporations and individual corporate managers?

The simplest answer, I think, is that too many business people think that fair competition is fine for the other person, but that their own interests somehow override everyone else's. (I once heard a high-level executive remark in a business meeting that he did not want a level playing ground; he always wanted an "edge.")

Now, let's consider several reported and hypothetical cases that are good examples of how the free market's operational rules may be violated and subject them to a moral analysis. It's important to note here that these cases concern actions that are or may be illegal, that Federal or state laws may be violated, but we're concerned with whether they are immoral.

LYING AND CHEATING?

The following examples are real cases from the 1980s:

1. . . . recently, E. F. Hutton & Company, one of the nation's largest brokerage firms, pleaded guilty to defrauding numerous small banks of millions of dollars through a check-kiting scheme that, in effect, gave the Wall Street house interest-free loans. E. F. Hutton has been fined $2 million and has agreed to repay to the banks the money it stole—perhaps $8 million.[1]

2. The military contracting arm of Litton Industries agreed to plead guilty to 325 counts of fraud for overbilling the Defense Department by $6.3 million, the largest case of false billing against a military contractor.[2]

3. The case cited in chapter 1 where a computer systems manufacturer bidding on a large government contract wasn't able to meet the date by which it was scheduled to demonstrate its system to the officials responsible for awarding the contract, and demonstrated another firm's system instead.

4. Consider a hypothetical case where a company includes in its bid equipment not yet commercially available—in direct violation of a requirement specified in the request for bids.

Moral Analysis

Kiting Checks. Let's examine the first case where a firm reportedly "kited" checks. The report doesn't give the details of how this particular scheme worked, so we'll examine a way it could be done, namely, by writing checks against funds scheduled for deposit but not yet deposited in one set of accounts and depositing those checks in turn in other accounts where they will earn interest. What, specifically, would be the problem here? Isn't it true that the temporary shortfall in the first set of accounts will likely be covered, perhaps in a matter of days? Don't the funds that are going to be deposited belong to the firm writing the checks?

In this hypothetical version of the scheme, the problem I see is that the money doesn't exist at the time the checks are written and deposited. The banks on which they are drawn could refuse to honor them, indicating "insufficient funds" to the institutions receiving the deposits; they, in turn, could refuse to credit the checks. That action would most likely be enough to stop the offending firm from continuing the practice.

The banks on which the checks were written could, of course, elect to ignore the overdrafts if the firm is a valued customer and then would be responsible for covering them. In that case, it seems like the funds really belong to the banks and any interest to be earned should be theirs. So, it looks like a firm kiting checks causes financial damage to the banks involved and, in effect, steals from them, although it might be argued that no stealing is involved if the banks go along with the scheme, even for reasons of expediency.

Overbilling. What about the action of a defense contractor that inflates its bills to the government? Is there any way to defend it? If the cost-padding is done just to add to the contractor's revenues, that is obviously theft: it is taking money to which he or she isn't entitled. But the reasoning and motivation at work here might be more subtle. The company might understate its costs in its bids just to insure winning the contract and either assume it can meet those costs or, once the work is underway and it would be difficult or impossible for the government agencies involved to stop it, assume it will be protected even if the understatement is discovered. Company officials could reason that a careful examination would show that their costs are probably not significantly if at all higher than the costs competitors would incur to provide the same product at the same levels of quality and efficiency. So the government can't really claim that it is being cheated.

The flaw in this reasoning, however, is that the government was lied to if the company submitted understated bids for the projects. It is reasonable to assume that an organization soliciting bids for work expects and is entitled to an honest statement of a contractor's capabilities and estimated costs. While a case can be made that unforeseen contingencies might generate higher expenses than originally anticipated, it would be wrong for a contractor to claim that it could do a job within a specified cost range knowing full well that it couldn't, even though it was sure that its end product would be completely satisfactory.

Deliberately understating estimated costs is also unfair to competitors who might have bid higher than the company that won the contract but would have actually delivered the product at a lower cost. In that case, the government would have been cheated as well because it could have gotten the product for less money if the bidding had been fair.

The Substitution. Consider next the case where the computer manufacturer was accused of substituting a different system for its own in order to meet a deadline for demonstrating its system's capabilities to a large government agency. What's wrong with that? Couldn't a manufacturer in this situation argue that it was reasonably sure its system would do the job to the agency's specifications? After all, what is being demonstrated is a capability, not specific hardware components. Besides, too much money is at stake to risk losing this kind of contract.

The point at issue, it seems to me, is that the government agency's representatives expected and had a right to see the system they were being offered in its entirety—including the hardware configuration. In my opinion, if a manufacturer's officials say "this is our system" when it isn't, they are purely and simply lying. They may be sure that their product will meet the bid specifications, but there is always the chance that its particular equipment configuration might not work. And, not least of all, rigging a demonstration in a case like this is unfair to competing bidders whose equipment is ready.

The firm described in the report did win the contract. However, when the Securities and Exchange Commission found out what happened, it accused the company of using fraudulent tactics. So the government, at least, seemed to think it was lied to.

Violating Bid Specifications. The moral judgment on the hypothetical company that includes equipment not commercially available at the time it submits its bid, in direct violation of the bidding specifications, seems pretty straightforward: its officials are purely and simply lying. An attempt to justify this kind of action might run along the line that the company is sure the equipment will be available when needed and the customer needn't worry on that score. But even if that is a reasonable assumption, the company violates an implicit contract since, if it is fully aware of the restriction, it accepts and agrees to it just by virtue of submitting its bid. An organization soliciting bids has a right to specify their conditions. No firm is obliged to accept them; it is free not to bid.

It would also be unfair to competitors for a company to violate this condition if competitors were able to meet a potential customer's specifications without relying on equipment that wasn't available at bid time.

MISREPRESENTING PRODUCT CONTENT

The following are more cases from the 1980s:

1. F.D.A. officials are worried that (drug) manufacturers may have substituted some ingredients in their drugs without approval. The officials said this could compromise the safety and effectiveness of a variety of medicines that are low-cost chemical copies of brand-name pharmaceuticals.[3]
2. Vitarine Pharmaceuticals Inc. . . . admitted giving false information in its application for the generic drug Dyazide, a copy of a blood pressure medicine . . . According to the F.D.A., Vitarine officials admitted that the data showing equivalence actually came from tests on the brand-named drug, not the generic.[4]
3. The former president of the Beech–Nut Nutrition Corporation admitted yesterday that he had knowingly sold sugar water to consumers who believed they were buying pure apple juice for their babies.[5]

What could be more straightforwardly a lie than substituting ingredients in a product for the ingredients it is supposed to contain? While everyone would agree, however, that it would be morally wrong to deliberately replace an ingredient with one that would cause harm, what's wrong with that substitution as long as the ingredient is harmless and customers are satisfied with what they get from the product? Babies who were fed water flavored with sugar and other additives instead of apple juice probably liked it. And, in the case of the drug manufacturer that admitted substituting test data from a brand-name drug for a generic drug for F.D.A. testing purposes, what harm was done as long as the generic substance was the equivalent of the brand-name product?

The answer is, I think, that buyers and sellers have agreed, at least implicitly, to a contract governing the marketplace: buyers are entitled to get what the seller tells them they are paying for. If a seller asserts that a product contains certain ingredients, he or she lies to the buyer if it in fact doesn't contain them. If the substitute causes harm to any of its buyers, the company is liable to the extent its managers knew about that possibility.

If a company substitutes test results from a brand-named drug for a generic drug for testing by the F.D.A., the rationale offered might be that both the company and the F.D.A. would save money by not having to go through a useless testing process. However, the public has stipulated, through its political agencies, that a condition of selling a drug that might be harmful is that it must go through F.D.A. testing. A drug manufacturer is not obliged to manufacture drugs if its managers think the testing requirement is too onerous and costly; but if the company wants to sell in the U.S. marketplace, it is bound to observe the rules. Ideally, at least, that's what the buyer expects and will enter into a purchasing contract only if that condition is met. To fail to observe the testing requirement is a violation of the contract's terms and is, it seems to me, unjust.

UNDERMINING THE BIDDING PROCESS

In an earlier chapter, we talked about a case where a government official pleaded guilty to receiving bribes for insider information he provided to consultants for firms bidding on government contracts and a case where a large corporation made payments to government officials in a foreign country in order to get a contract for its airplanes. Kickbacks and facilitating payments seem to be a common business practice.

Companies commonly request bids from suppliers for a myriad of products and services. These bids are often sealed so that only designated company officials will open them, and no one will tamper with them. The intent of the process is, of course, to obtain competitive bids so that the best (not necessarily the lowest) price will be obtained along with a quality product delivered within an acceptable time-frame. Theoretically, any supplier with the capability of meeting the bid specifications has an equal opportunity with all other suppliers to present its case for winning the contract.

There are a number of ways to interfere with this process: bribes may be used to influence managers responsible for selecting suppliers; someone within the company may leak information about other competitors' bids to one or more of the competitors; a company may knowingly favor its own subsidiary company without letting the other competitors know that. These actions attack the very essence of the bidding procedure. Managers who engage in them risk cheating their companies (or, in the case of U.S. Government contracts, the taxpayers) because added costs may result (sometimes to cover the cost of kickbacks or bribes), or the company's reputation might suffer because it couldn't produce the best quality product in the specified time-frames. The implicit contract between the organizations requesting bids and responding suppliers is violated by these actions: the suppliers make bids in good faith, expecting that their offers will be judged on their merits. That is the way the game is supposed to be played in a free-enterprise, openly competitive capitalistic society, and everyone is expected to know and play by that rule. That's why, for example, the manager who leaks a bid in the expectation of forcing one bidder to a lower price acts unjustly toward all the other bidders even though he or she thinks that the leak is to the company's advantage. The rules are violated by giving one bidder access to information it's not supposed to have.

Further, it is patently unfair to ask bidders to incur the expense of preparing and submitting a bid when there is no chance of its being accepted. It is unjust to solicit bids for any reason other than a bona fide request: for instance, merely to meet Equal Opportunity requirements, or just to reassure higher management that sufficient bids are being solicited. That's why it would be unjust for a company to ask for bids when it knows that the contract will go to one of its subsidiaries and it fails to tell the other bidders that a subsidiary may be favored.

Managers who accept kickbacks from suppliers might in fact obtain reliable products from them, but they are certainly vulnerable to future pressures and probable conflicts of interest from those firms. It would be a rare company that would not tell its managers that using inside information or taking kickbacks could result in severe disciplinary action, up to and including dismissal, even if those methods appeared to benefit the company in a particular situation.

PRICE–FIXING

Consider two reported cases:

1. An executive of a company pleaded guilty to conspiring to fix the prices of his firm's products ("Coke Exec," 1987).
2. Forty-seven executives of cardboard box manufacturers who had pleaded no contest to charges of rigging prices in the folding carton industry were given jail terms and fines today.[6]

Are price-fixing and collusion on allocating market shares really morally wrong? How can anyone claim that consumers have a moral right to the best quality products and services at the least possible cost? Why aren't vendors entitled to work out whatever systems will provide the greatest return on their hard work and ingenuity?

I think the argument has to begin with recalling what the free-enterprise market is all about. Ideally, the market is open to anyone who wants to offer a product or service at whatever price he or she thinks will move it and will pick up a profitable share of the market from competitors. That means that buyers will pay the lowest possible price for any commodity because those vendors who can supply it efficiently and at a high level of equality (maybe because they work harder or are more skilled at what they do) will be able to underprice those who are less efficient or competent. Competition in the free market is supposed to insure the best quality products for the consumer at the lowest possible prices.

The practice of fixing prices and allocating market shares among competitors destroys the free-market dynamics. It discourages innovation and inevitably results in higher prices for consumers. But why is that necessarily immoral?

First of all, when the political system in which buyers and sellers operate has established that the market is to be free and competitive so that its members will pay a minimal amount for quality goods and services and innovation and invention will be stimulated, a contract is established between buyers and sellers—at least implicitly. If entrepreneurs want to sell in that market, they have to observe its pricing structure. Price-fixing and market collusion violate that contract and are, therefore, unjust.

Second, as I have frequently pointed out, the economic system is supposed to provide human beings access to the resources needed to live in decent, humane, conditions that provide opportunity for personal growth and development. To the extent that market-rigging restricts that access, it violates human dignity—especially when necessities of life like shelter, food, education, and health may be priced beyond some people's ability to pay for them.

Finally, product innovation and quality are at least threatened by price-fixing; why, for instance, should a company spend significant resources on research and development when its markets and profits are assured? It's not immediately evident to me that there is necessarily something immoral about delaying innovation, that consumers have a right to it. There is the argument in support of that right that all technology and inventions belong to the community in the sense that the people who developed them received their education from the community and have built their own work on the work of inventors and innovators who preceded them. So their inventions are not their own in any absolute sense. Or, perhaps it could be argued that delays in innovation violate the contract between buyers and sellers that the political system established when it adopted a free-market economic structure. In effect, a contractual condition of entering the market is, at very least, staying open to the possibility of rapid product innovation. But I think it would be very difficult for political authorities to know when to step in and compel innovation except by laws prohibiting behavior like forming cartels or engaging in other monopolistic practices specifically designed to restrict or delay it.

THE UTILITARIAN APPROACH

A natural-law moralist who clearly identifies any of the actions in the cases and situations just discussed as instances of lying, cheating, or stealing, considers it intrinsically wrong and, therefore, forbidden. While the action may be more or less evil depending on the greater or lesser malice or harm it involves, still, for this moralist, no situation or set of circumstances can ever justify doing such an action.

The moral analysis I offered on these cases relied heavily on notions of rights, justice, human dignity, and other arguments from natural-law moral theory. In effect, they overrode a simple comparison of the overall good and bad consequences generated by these actions that I labeled as instances of fraud of some kind. But could a utilitarian case be made for justifying any of them?

The most significant challenge to the utilitarian argument would come from the theory's key tenet that the good of the agent (in these cases, companies) does not, by itself, count for more than the good of the other parties concerned. Even if actions like kiting checks, substituting another company's computer system for one's own in a competitive bidding situation, understating costs and overbilling on government contracts, misrepresenting one's ability to meet bid specifications, leaking bids to competing suppliers, paying bribes to representatives of companies soliciting bids, misrepresenting product content, and colluding on prices and market shares would significantly promote the interests of the stockholders, employees, and social and political communities depending on the companies doing these things, it would have to be shown that these interests would outweigh the interests of the shareholders, employees, and social and political communities of competing companies and of society, overall.

I think a utilitarian moralist would have a hard time making that case. My guess is that he or she would arrive at pretty much the same moral judgments I did using a nonutilitarian approach.

Price-fixing might be one exception. A utilitarian could argue that fixing prices and allocating certain kinds of markets among several large companies would insure that their profits were kept high enough to provide good dividends, good salaries, benefits, and long-term tenure for employees, and good economic and tax situations for the political entities in which the companies operated. Fragmenting the market by allowing many smaller companies to enter it, companies that most likely could not pay the same level of salaries and benefits or taxes, might ultimately result in fewer jobs, lower salaries and dividends, and worse economic conditions for their political communities. Oligopolies, then, at least in certain industries, might be better overall for everybody than a completely free competitive market. But a utilitarian would have to show that when measured against the higher prices for consumers, costlier products, less innovation and development and, possibly, restricted access to the commodities some people need just to exist in minimally decent conditions, the good consequences generated by oligopolies clearly would outweigh the bad ones. And even if they did, it would seem that the political system's approval would be required, just as it is in the case of monopolies like public utilities. If the community agreed to allow oligopolies, that decision would not be immoral, provided no one was denied access to necessary resources as a result.

THE CULTURAL RELATIVIST'S APPROACH

All of the cases and situations just presented probably represent areas where the cultural relativist's approach to moral issues is, in my experience, most appealing to many business people. In the absence of laws specifically addressing contract and bidding procedures, bribery and kickbacks, banking, price-fixing, and the content of food and drugs, the familiar injunctions like "do what's customary" or "let the buyer beware" have a strong appeal.

Even where there are laws against the practices described in the cases, however, there is often an attitude that because "everybody does it" or "it has to be done to stay in business" (because competitors are going to do it anyway, and I'm as deserving of the business as they are), these laws should be disregarded. This is especially true when such laws in a society are widely, persistently, and consistently evaded by its members. Many business people are particularly fond of defending bribes or kickback payments in foreign countries, for instance, by claiming that these practices are the way business is done, are the "way of life" there—even though these kinds of payments are against the law in all countries (Noonan, 1984).

Assuming that the cultural relativist truly wants to act morally, how does he or she resolve the conflict between law and practice? How would he or she approach all the cases we've discussed here?

The logic of the moral relativist's position demands that he or she determine to the extent possible what the mores of the society in which he or she is doing business really do dictate about the transactions we've discussed in the cases. If there are laws governing them, and unless it can be shown that a particular law has been drafted purely in the selfish interest of certain individuals or corporations against the general preference of a society, the cultural relativist must, I believe, accept those laws as the expression of the society's mores and must be morally bound to observe them—no matter how many of his or her fellow business people may disregard them.

SUMMARY

The free-enterprise, capitalistic, economic system has, according to its advocates, produced the highest standard of living for more people than any other economic system. The inherent strength of the system is said to stem from

- the free-market where buyers and sellers exchange goods and services at prices freely negotiated;

- the efficient allocation of resources it ensures by providing only what buyers want;
- the wide variety of products it makes available to buyers;
- the distribution of financial rewards to those who work harder and more ingeniously than others;
- the reliance on open competition that drives prices as low as possible for the consumer and eliminates unfair advantages among producers;
- the prosperity it provides directly or indirectly to all members of the society in which the free market operates.

So goes the theory of the free market, capitalistic economy. But why is there so much ethical misconduct evident in so many of its day-to-day operations, at least in the United States where it is seen as paradigmatic?

The simplest answer to that question is that many business people are all for a competitive market for the other person, but insist on an edge for their own interests.

We considered several actual or hypothetical cases illustrating the kinds of violations of the free-market system that occur and argued that a natural-law moralist would find any action determined to be an instance of lying, cheating, or stealing intrinsically immoral and forbidden—no matter how many good consequences it might generate.

This moralist might find instances of these failures in the cases we looked at involving actions like check-kiting (in one version, earning interest on money that belongs to someone else), substituting another firm's equipment for one's own in a competitive bidding situation (an apparent instance of a direct lie), overbilling the government (apparently, simply pocketing money to which one is not entitled), and, hypothetically, including in bids equipment not commercially available—in direct violation of bidding specifications (probably, a direct lie to a customer and an injustice to competitors who didn't do this in their bids).

We examined instances of substituting content in drugs (a potential threat to the user or to the drug's effectiveness), substituting test results from a brand-name drug for a generic drug being tested by the F.D.A. (an apparent instance of lying), and putting sugar-water in a baby-food product labeled as apple juice (not providing what the manufacturer said it was providing, and, as a result, deceiving customers).

Cases where the bidding process was undermined were discussed. I argued that these actions, on natural-law grounds, were immoral on several counts. Managers who pay bribes risk cheating their companies by adding the costs of bribes to the cost of their product. They also risk their company's reputation if they can't produce the best-quality product in the time-frames specified by the contract. Competitors are harmed because they make bids in good faith expecting to have their offers judged on their merits.

A special case of unfair treatment in letting out bids is to ask firms to prepare and submit them just to satisfy legal requirements or to make upper management believe that bids are being solicited properly when there is no chance these bids will be considered.

Finally, managers who accept kickbacks become vulnerable to future pressures and probable conflicts of interest from those firms who paid them.

Cases involving price-fixing were examined. Price-fixing was judged immoral because it violated the dynamics to which all parties in the free-market system have explicitly or implicitly agreed; it is a violation of the contract among buyers and sellers that the system will be used to produce the lowest-priced, best quality merchandise and will stimulate product innovation.

It was suggested that price-fixing threatens product innovation because no company will want to innovate as long as profits on its current products are guaranteed. It has to be established, of course, that consumers have a right to innovation. One argument for this right might be that all technology and inventions belong to some extent to the community because the community educated its inventors and innovators. Further, the fact that inventors and innovators depended on the work of those who preceded them might support the right of the public to innovation in products.

The utilitarian case for justifying the actions of the managers involved in all these cases in terms of the overall good consequences that might be generated was challenged on the grounds that these actions done in the interests of one company's shareholders, employees, and social and political communities would always outweigh the interests of the corresponding parties in other companies. It was suggested that the utilitarian moralist would have a hard time making that case.

The one exception for the utilitarian might be price-fixing, where collusion among companies would insure high profits for them and in turn insure high dividends for shareholders, good salaries and benefits for employees, and good economic and tax situations for their political entities. But the utilitarian would have to show that these benefits would truly offset the higher prices for consumers, less product innovation and development, and, possibly, restricted access to commodities some people might need to live in minimally decent conditions. It would seem that the political communities involved would have to approve any oligopolies that would result from price-fixing to insure that they were in fact operating in the public interest.

All of the cases presented represent areas where cultural relativism might have the greatest appeal. "Do what's customary" or "let the buyer beware" are common injunctions that might be offered by some business people where there are no laws covering contracts and bidding, bribery and kickbacks, banking, price-fixing and the content of food and drugs. Even where laws do apply, they are often persistently and consistently evaded because "everybody does it" or "it has to be done to stay in business." Bribes and kickbacks, in particular, are often defended as the "way of life" even in countries where the law forbids them.

The logic of the cultural relativist's position requires him or her to determine what society's laws or customs dictate about the kinds of transactions discussed in the cases. If there are laws governing them, it seems to me that the cultural relativist has to obey them—no matter how flagrantly others may ignore them.

NOTES

1. Schanberg, S. H. "Color Accountability Gray," *The New York Times*, May 14, 1985, p. A27. Copyright © 1985 by The New York Times. Reprinted by permission.

2. Gruson, L. "Litton Unit to Pay $15 Million to U.S.," *The New York Times*, July 16, 1986, pp. A1, D4. Copyright © 1986 by The New York Times. Reprinted by permission.

3. Andrews, E. L. "F.D.A. Inquiry on Generic Drugs Focuses on Switch of Ingredients," *The New York Times*, July 31, 1989, pp. A1, A10. Copyright © 1989 by The New York Times. Reprinted by permission.

4. Ibid.

5. "Guilty Plea by Ex-Officer of Beech-Nut," *The New York Times*, November 14, 1989, pp. D1, D4. Copyright © 1989 by The New York Times. Reprinted by permission.

6. "47 Box Executives draw Jail and Fines for Rigging Prices," *The New York Times*, December 1, 1976, pp. A1, D9. Copyright © 1976 by The New York Times. Reprinted by permission.

13

Advertising

ADVERTISING IN THE FREE–ENTERPRISE SYSTEM

"It pays to advertise" is practically a truism in a free-enterprise, competitive economic system. Few, if any, businesses can move their wares in the market without letting potential customers know what they have to sell, and customers cannot make informed, free choices of products and services unless they know what's out there. Advertising, then, is an essential instrument of communication between sellers and buyers.

Advertising fosters competition. Small businesses often use it to get into markets that may be dominated by economic oligarchies and to generate competitive pressures that will tend to drive prices down in those markets. To the extent that advertising attracts more customers to a particular item, its price may be lowered because increased demand often reduces the cost of producing each unit of the item, and that saving may be passed on to customers in the form of lower prices.

There is nothing morally wrong, then, with the practice of advertising in itself, but how managers advertise may generate moral problems. These problems usually center around the use of persuasion and the creation of consumer demands.

PERSUASION

Managers use advertising not just to let people know what they have to sell but to *persuade* consumers to buy their wares. Moral questions may arise sometimes because of the way advertisers go about trying to convince people that they should buy their products. The following are some examples.

- A company may make out-and-out-false claims about its products.
- Some scientific studies claim that smoking causes lung cancer. But despite the evidence offered by these studies and the U.S. Surgeon General's warnings on the dangers of smoking, tobacco companies continue to use advertising media to persuade people that smoking is pleasurable and even, perhaps, sophisticated. These ads might lead some people, especially young people, to ignore the health warnings and take up smoking or continue to smoke.
- Many forms of advertising rely on appeals to vanity and health claims.
- Ads frequently use sexual innuendo for their persuasive impact and are often considered offensive by the public.
- Manufacturers of plastic bags used for garbage and trash disposal advertised them as biodegradable. Consumers might have inferred that the bags were environmentally safe, but that was true only if the bags were exposed to sunlight. Since most of these bags are buried in landfills and will probably never see the sun, the inference that they would degrade naturally was unsound.
- Toy companies advertise extensively on TV programs directed at children, apparently relying on the children to persuade their parents to buy toys.

WHAT MORALITY REQUIRES OF ADVERTISERS

The fundamental moral principle governing advertising is to tell the truth. Potential customers have the right to know what a product may legitimately be expected to accomplish for them. Ads that make outright false claims about products or services are simply instances of lying. They are straightforwardly immoral because they blatantly defraud customers and are unfair to honest competitors.

The same is true for ads that mislead, although they may be harder to identify. All advertising is designed to attract attention, and it is here that the temptation to exaggerate is probably most often encountered.

APPEALS TO HALF–TRUTHS

Here are some examples of advertising practices that skate perilously close to the edge of deception:

- oversize packaging of small amounts of a product to make it look like the customer is getting a lot for his or her money;
- "going out of business" sales that last indefinitely;
- advertising sales that aren't really sales at all or that extend over a suspiciously long time;
- "bait and switch" ads that promise low prices on quality merchandise that is sold out or not available for some other reason when customers come into the store to buy it. Lower-quality or higher-priced merchandise is then offered as a substitute.

APPEALS TO HUMAN VANITY

Are appeals to human vanity straightforwardly immoral? Not necessarily. Take the fact that most of us want to present a good appearance in public. It's possible that products like grooming aids, deodorants, cosmetics, or health aids designed to heal or cover up physical blemishes like acne may in fact enhance people's appearances and eliminate one source of their anxieties.

CELEBRITY ENDORSEMENTS

Celebrities in various walks of life often promote products. A person might infer that because celebrities are who they are, what they are endorsing must be good. If a celebrity or the models used in ads are beautiful, handsome, sexually appealing, athletic, healthy, or obviously happy people, and are touting some beauty or grooming aid, cosmetic, item of clothing, food, health remedy, vehicle, or recreational activity, a few gullible people might be led to think that the product will help make them more beautiful, handsome, sexually appealing, athletic, healthy, or less anxious and happy too.

Is it immoral to use celebrities to persuade people to buy a product? Probably not. It's reasonable to assume that most people are well aware that using certain products will not necessarily make them look like movie stars or athletes or act like wealthy entrepreneurs, and they understand that the sole value of ads featuring these people is really just to call attention to a product, not to directly mislead or lie to consumers.

It's another story, of course, if advertisers intend to deceive or manipulate people with these ads. A natural-law moralist for whom intention is important in making moral judgments would condemn any ad whose objective is deception or manipulation or an attempt to subvert the freedom of consumers—like subliminal advertising where a message is allegedly flashed to viewers and perceived below the level of their immediate consciousness but that is nevertheless intended to affect their choices. Ads that are deliberately manipulative by playing on the anxieties or feelings of inadequacy of some people (like teenagers who are self-conscious about acne) and unduly affect their ability to choose freely would also be morally suspect, I think, for this moralist. The bad intention alone would be enough to vitiate these kinds of advertising even if the intended effects didn't occur.

A utilitarian moralist would not be concerned with the intentions of the advertisers in these cases but only with whether or not this kind of advertising produced good consequences overall.

A cultural relativist would rely on whatever laws governed advertising practices or would follow whatever society accepted in the world of advertising.

What about the moral responsibility of the celebrities themselves who appear in ads endorsing products? Are they acting immorally if they really don't believe in or even use the products whose value they are attesting to? Are they lying to consumers? I'm sure they would argue that they are just working, "acting" as it were, and don't expect people to believe that they are personally sold on the virtues of the items they are touting. They probably see their role as simply communicating the availability of the product and what its manufacturer says it will do for people. They likely assume that the general public realizes this and doesn't really think that actors necessarily believe in what they are helping advertise.

Their argument is probably valid, for the most part. Of course, they are lying if their endorsement of the product definitely depends on their using it but they really don't use it.

PRESSURE ON SELECTED AUDIENCES

Using ads to appeal to pressure an audience that is not mature enough to see through them, like children, is simply deceptive. Advertising that is specifically designed to manipulate children and use them to pressure parents to buy toys, for example, is immoral because it violates their dignity as persons; it takes unfair advantage of their immaturity. That doesn't mean that all advertising directed at children is automatically immoral. After all, they are the target audience for toy manufacturers; who else can the toy manufacturers effectively address?

Parents, of course, are the ultimate marketing target because they hold the purse strings, and it would be naive to believe that they are not influenced by their children's wants. But as long as the advertising simply presents the attractiveness of the toys in themselves, it's hard to see why that is immoral. What would be immoral would be to deliberately take advantage of children's immaturity and manipulate their wants by implying, for instance, that they will necessarily be happier, perhaps more successful in school, or more socially acceptable if they own and play with certain toys or entertain their playmates with them.

ADVERTISING THAT DEMEANS PEOPLE

Advertising that demeans human dignity is immoral. The blatant use of sexual innuendo is a case in point, because it exploits and degrades a significant and profoundly personal human experience by reducing it to just another way to hawk wares. Advertising may also be sexist; it may, for example, imply that men are attracted only to women who use a particular product, or dress in a particular fashion or are as slender as fashion models, or that women will certainly be attracted to men who use certain shaving lotions or cologne or deodorants. It's not that people will necessarily be taken in by this kind of message; it's the way the message is conveyed that may degrade either sex, for example, by implying that all men or all women are naturally stupid about certain fashions, appliances, sports or, just because they are men or women, that they are inordinately vain.

IS ADVERTISING RESPONSIBLE FOR CONSUMERISM AND MATERIALISM?

Some religious leaders warn that consumerism and materialism, construed as measures of excess, are a threat to people's spiritual lives.[1] Since advertising probably does create desires for more and better and newer things and people often go into debt to get them, is advertising the culprit in promoting these two "isms?"

It must be remembered, I think, that advertising is very nearly an essential component of a free-enterprise economic system, a system that is expected to provide access to resources in such a way that everyone in the society it serves can lead a reasonably decent, comfortable life. Since consumption is necessary for our survival, it obviously keeps any economic system going. Advertising contributes to consumption, so it's not too far-fetched to believe that in the end, advertising serves human welfare.

Consumerism and materialism, defined as an excess or insatiable desire to amass more and more things or to cater to human appetites, are morally questionable, but consumption is not. Consumption is about using material resources for the welfare of human beings. True, human dignity is diminished by an inordinate need to have more and more material possessions, but when anyone's preference for material things outweighs his or her preference for spiritual values, that aberration is likely attributable to something in the person's character, and it would be wrong to blame advertising for it. In itself, advertising is at least morally neutral, and the moral limits placed on it are that it may not use any of the illicit ploys we already talked about. Most importantly, it has to respect the freedom of individuals to make their own unpressured choices about the goods and services they will buy. As long as advertisers observe these limits in their advertising practices, they shouldn't hesitate to tell the world about their products and services and try to persuade people to buy them.

SUMMARY

Advertising is an essential instrument of communication between buyers and sellers. It lets customers know what's out there in the market and helps sellers move their wares. It fosters competition that tends to drive prices down because increased demand often reduces the cost of producing an item, and these savings may be passed on to customers in the form of lower prices.

There is nothing wrong with advertising in itself, but how advertisers attempt to create demand and persuade customers to buy may generate moral problems. Some advertisers have made false or misleading claims about their products. Others use appeals to human vanity, health, and use sexual innuendo (often seen by the public as offensive), or what looks like undue pressure on some segment of the market to persuade people to buy.

The fundamental moral principle governing advertising is that customers have a right to know the truth about the products they buy, what the products will in fact do for them. Therefore, ads that make false claims are simply lies. They defraud customers and are unfair to honest competitors. Misleading advertising, although harder to identify, sometimes, falls into the same moral category.

Examples of half-truths used in advertising are deliberate oversize packaging of products, "going out of business" sales that last indefinitely, advertised sales that aren't really sales at all, and "bait and switch" ads that lure customers into a store where a pitch is made for an item different from that advertised or for a better quality model of the item—all at a higher price than was originally advertised.

Celebrities often promote products. A few people might draw the conclusion that since people who are beautiful, handsome, sexually appealing, athletic, healthy or obviously happy people endorse a particular product, some of those qualities might rub off on them if they were to use it. It was suggested that this kind of advertising is not straightforwardly immoral because it's reasonable to assume that most people really know that these products will not make them look or act like these celebrities and understand that the only reason celebrities appear in these ads is to attract attention to the products. It would be immoral, however, if a celebrity deliberately left the impression that he or she really believed in or used a product if that was not in fact the case.

A natural-law moralist would find any ad immoral where the advertiser deliberately intends to deceive people—whether the deception actually occurs or not. Ads that undermine free choice, such as messages delivered subliminally or ads that deliberately appeal to or manipulate the anxieties of people, would likely be morally suspect for this moralist.

The utilitarian would be concerned with whether or not any advertising practice produced more good consequences than bad ones. The cultural relativist would look to the law or whatever advertising practices society was accustomed to tolerate if no laws applied.

Ads that are deliberately designed to manipulate children, to take advantage of their immaturity and get them to put pressure on their parents to buy toys are immoral because they violate children's dignity as persons. Ads designed to call attention to the attractiveness of toys are not immoral in themselves; it's selling the idea to the children that the toys will necessarily make them happier or more successful in school or more socially acceptable to their playmates that seems morally wrong.

Advertising that demeans human dignity by sexual innuendo is immoral because it degrades a significant and profoundly personal human experience. Sexist advertising that implies that men or women will be attracted only to members of the opposite sex who use a particular product is morally questionable to the extent that the way the message is conveyed degrades either sex by implying that men or women are just naturally stupid in certain areas or are inordinately vain.

Advertising is criticized by some religious leaders because it promotes consumerism and materialism. It prompts people to want more and more things. In rebuttal, however, it was argued that advertising is necessary to a free-enterprise economic system; without consumption there will be no economic activity and advertising contributes to consumption.

The inordinate appetite to amass more and more things is morally questionable, but advertising in itself is not. An inordinate preference for material over spiritual things is probably attributable to a person's character, and advertising should not take the blame for it.

Advertising, I conclude, is morally neutral in itself, and as long as advertisers respect people's freedom to make unpressured choices about goods and services, advertisers are perfectly justified in telling people, even persuasively, what they have to sell.

NOTE

1. Pope John Paul II, e.g., in his Encyclical Letter, *Centesimus Annus*, May 1, 1991, paragraph 19.

14

Closing Down an Operation

A PLANT CLOSES

A few years ago, the Chrysler Corporation decided to close down one of its plants that had been operating in a community for over 30 years. Although the plant ranked well in productivity compared with the company's other plants, the reason management gave for closing it was overcapacity; the demand for the particular models produced there was down.

As might be expected, the news of the closing was a shock to the community because of its devastating economic impact. Over 4,000 jobs would be lost. A large number of the employees being terminated had put in over 20 years of service, and their chances to earn better pensions based on longer service were obviously jeopardized. The community's tax base would be eroded; property values would drop; supporting businesses, industries, and religious and cultural institutions from food stores to parochial schools would be severely affected.

Critics of the closing claimed that the company was acting unjustly toward the community because it had violated a contract made 31 years ago when it began operations there. Roads and schools were built and police and fire services probably expanded with tax money; churches undertook building programs; small businesses and industries were established in support of the company and its workers. Workers signed on with the company and bought houses and began to raise families. All of this activity was probably undertaken with the expectation and understanding that the plant would be there indefinitely, and that the community could count on its long-term commitment.

Critics also doubted that the company's basic rationale for the closing, overcapacity, was legitimate in view of the fact that it had opened new plants in foreign countries. They suspected that some of the vehicles produced there would find their way back into the United States.

Finally, critics pointed out that the workers had no say in the decision to close the plant (Windsor, 1990).

Are the arguments offered by the critics sound? Let's establish a hypothetical third-person dialogue between plant officials and the community and examine these arguments critically.

We'll begin with the idea of a "contract" the community might claim was made with it when the plant opened. Unless there was some sort of formal written agreement entered into with city officials, it was at best implicit. But what could such a contract guarantee? Did the fact that the plant was built in that particular community automatically constitute a promise that the company would never leave? Did the employees who signed up to work at the plant automatically establish a claim to long-term employment, wages, and benefits?

The company, it may be presumed, would argue in rebuttal that it never offered guarantees of that kind. It probably located where it did for many reasons: the community might have offered a good source of dependable workers and easy access to the transportation facilities needed to bring in raw materials and deliver finished products; it may have been attractive to managers who would have to transfer and make their homes there because it had good schools, shopping, and recreational facilities; its political climate may have been favorable to business. But, at best, the company could only guarantee that it would remain in the community as long as its operation there was profitable. Surely the community's political, social, religious, and cultural leaders and the owners of supporting businesses and industries had to understand that. After all, in a free-market economic system, buyers and sellers are free to enter and leave the market as they see fit. At the time of locating the plant, all predictions may have indicated the likelihood that it would operate for a long time, but that could never have been assured independently of economic conditions that could change drastically. No company can afford to operate a plant indefinitely at a loss; eventually, unprofitable operations have to be shut down. So the company surely would reject the idea that it had entered into any kind of contract with the community. Besides, the company had stayed in the community for 30 years—certainly not a fly-by-night commitment by any means.

Finally, the company might have suggested that the political and social organizations in the community owed it a great deal. The income available to the community's members to care for health needs, educate their children, support their religious programs, and enjoy recreational and cultural activities was largely generated, directly or indirectly, by the plant. It was likely that the company had donated generously to cultural and social organizations over the years. Its managers and employees may have assumed leadership roles in numerous civic enterprises like United Way campaigns, youth organizations, church committees and local government bodies.

The community's leaders would probably respond to this rebuttal by stressing several points. First, when a company starts up an operation in a community, it is well aware that political and social entities will incur costs to support it. Tax rebates may have been offered to attract the company to the community. Roads, sewage systems, schools, libraries, service, and protective services will likely be expanded, and these costs may be laid directly at the doorstep of the company. Unless the company were to pay outright for all of them, members of the community pay some share of these costs. That all these amenities are in place serves the company's interests if only in terms of insuring its ability to attract and retain managers and employees. That's one reason the company "owes" the community. Nor will all taxes assessed on the company pay just for the expense incurred on its behalf because as a member of the community, the company is also a citizen and is obliged to pay a share of the ongoing costs needed to insure that the community will provide an environment that will contribute to its members' welfare.

Second, the company knows full well that employees who build homes and establish families near the place they work are assuming some sort of long-term financial stability from their employer in terms of wages and benefits. Why else would they incur protracted financial obligations?

Third, the businesses established to serve the new market provided by the company and its employees are under no obligation to invest in the community; but many of these businesses do serve the plant's operation directly, and indirectly, of course, by the services they offer its employees. It seems like the company owes them something, too.

Finally, while the community's members obviously benefit from the company's payroll, as devoted and hard-working employees they contribute directly to the company's success. What they receive in wages, they earn. And while the company's managers and employees may contribute much time and effort to leadership roles in the community's organizations, they and their families also benefit from the services offered by those same organizations.

In view of its awareness of all kinds of expectations on the part of employees and of the relationships established with political, social, and business entities, a company surely knows that its commitment to an operation in a community must be long-term.

In the specific case we are considering, the second challenge to the company's decision to close the plant was that it had opened new plants in foreign countries; therefore, the claim of overcapacity was spurious. Further, it could be argued, if the vehicles produced in the foreign plants did show up in the U.S. market, jobs belonging to American workers had in effect been exported to foreigners willing to work for lower wages and benefits.

The company might have responded to this point by pointing out that it has a primary fiduciary responsibility to earn a profit for its shareholders. This U.S. plant was no longer profitable because demand for the models made there was down, but they could be made, perhaps, at a profit overseas. Further, people in those countries also have a right to access resources on behalf of themselves and their families, and the company was really killing two birds with one stone: generating profits for shareholders and providing jobs for people in underdeveloped countries. Finally, it was probably unlikely that vehicles produced in the foreign countries would replace those produced in the closing plant on a one-to-one basis; so American jobs weren't really being replaced. (And, even if the company had no intention of importing any of the vehicles produced in those plants to the United States, there still might be a lesson here for U.S. workers: if they and the companies they work for plan to remain competitive, especially in the international market, salaries and benefits may need to be reduced to compete with what foreign workers receive.)

The third criticism of the company's decision was that the employees had no voice in it. A totalitarian-like action was taken that would have serious economic and psychological effects on human beings; it's no small matter, after all, to take away a person's livelihood, jeopardize his or her life plans for self and family, and contribute to the possible destruction of his or her religious and civic organizations without any consultation with the person beforehand. Such an action is an extreme violation of human dignity.

The company's rejoinder would likely have been to point out that these employees had no right of ownership in the company and, consequently, no say in decisions that affect its organizational structure and fundamental mode of operation. Decisions at that level belong to the owners of the company, its shareholders, and are entrusted by them to the managers they have appointed to run it. The employees' say in the operation of the company is limited to those policies, procedures, wages, and benefit decisions that management agrees are open to discussion with them, either by management directive or by contract with the union.

Let's see whether we can derive some practical principles from the valid points made in these hypothetical arguments and counter-arguments and try to further derive some conclusions about the moral limits on closing down a company's operations in a community.

Given a political system which endorses a competitive, free-market economic system, where profit is the *sine qua non* of any ongoing private economic enterprise, no business can commit itself unreservedly to an indefinite operation in any given community. It is always vulnerable to conditions beyond its control. Consider just a few simple examples:

- The natural resources on which its operation depends like coal, gas, or oil, for instance, may simply be depleted.

- The market for its product may disappear. Nobody, for instance, is interested in buying asbestos insulation anymore.

- Even though the company's managers might agree that the employees deserve their wage and benefit bill, the company's revenues and level of efficiency may not be sufficient to meet it and still turn an acceptable profit.

- State or local taxes may be so high that the company cannot pay them and also earn a reasonable profit. This could well be true in the case of small, marginal operations.

- Government regulations like environmental protection restrictions may make it impossible to deliver a product at a price consumers are willing to pay. Large manufacturers may be able to survive, but smaller ones might have to close down.

The employees of a particular business and the members of the community where it is located must be aware of and understand these limitations, especially if they themselves are committed to a free-market, competitive economic system. (If they're not, they need to establish a political system that won't allow it.) They must be aware that they are taking some risk when going to work for a particular company or offering that company tax or wage incentives to locate in their community. It's also likely true that the smaller the company or the more restricted or specialized its product, the greater that risk may be. Employees also need to recognize that the company's shareholders are exercising their moral right to access material resources through their ownership of their company's assets and are entitled to a reasonable return on their investment.

A company that establishes an operation in a community, especially if it does so as a result of political or labor-related incentives that may have been offered to it, surely understands that its employees and the members of the community have some legitimate long-term economic expectations about it. They expect to exercise their moral right to access material resources through their employment in the company. The company cannot exist purely to generate profits for its owners; in the wider social context it is a mechanism for people other than the owners to meet their economic needs. A company also knows full well that the community will incur long-term costs in terms of roads, schools, sewage treatment systems, and other supporting services and institutions that will serve the company's operation. Both the company and the community will benefit from these expenditures, and each has to pay its fair share. So, while a company may not make a formal, iron-clad contract that it will remain in a location for a long period of time, it makes an indirect commitment to stay there as long as it is profitable. That condition is an important qualifier, of course, because no one is held to the impossible. An operation that can't make a profit cannot stay in existence indefinitely.

A company, by virtue of settling in a community, becomes a member of it. That means that its owners and managers have an obligation to support the structures needed by the community to promote the welfare of its members. The company is obliged to pay its fair share of taxes and should be willing to support, as a matter of philanthropy, educational and cultural programs not furnished out of the public treasury. (Corporate executives commonly describe their companies as "good corporate citizens," so this is usually not seen as an unreasonable burden, at least by large companies.)

MORAL LIMITS ON CLOSING DOWN A COMPANY'S OPERATIONS

What might we conclude now about the moral limits on closing down a company's operations in a community?

No company is obliged to remain in a community when the company clearly can no longer sustain a profitable operation there. However, if the profit turndown is short-term and the company has profitable operations elsewhere, they should carry the loser until its own profitability is restored—assuming that to be a likely expectation.

Unless it has explicitly let it be known from the beginning that its operation will last for a limited time in a location, a company does have some long-term commitment to its employees and the community in which it operates, as long as it can sustain a reasonable level of profitability there. It would be morally questionable, therefore, for a company to shut down an operation just because the company could pay lower wages and benefits in some other location and could pay higher dividends to its shareholders as a result. While shareholders do have a right to access material resources for their needs through their ownership of businesses, that right is limited by the rights of others to that same access. It is true that a company exists to produce profits for its owners, but, in the larger context of social and distributive justice in a free-market economic system, it exists to provide for other people working in and living under that system as well.

For these reasons, it would be unjust for a company to move an operation to a foreign country and substitute foreign workers for its domestic workers just to maximize its stockholders' earnings. There is nothing wrong with investing in a foreign country and operating there at lower wage and benefit costs and earning dividends for shareholders; people in other countries have a right to use resources in their own and their families' interests. But they should not obtain their jobs by directly replacing workers in another country. It would also be morally questionable, I think, for a company to replace, on a one-to-one basis, its products made in a domestic operation with the same products made in a foreign country, if doing that would result in a loss of domestic jobs.

While it is true that employees do not (unless they are shareholders) own the companies they work for and cannot have the definitive say in whether an operation should shut down or not, respect for their dignity as persons demands that they be heard from on a decision that will profoundly affect their lives. They certainly need some advance notice so that they can begin to plan for what has to be a traumatic experience.

At the very least, the company has to listen to its employees' objections, consider their economic needs, and hear out any possible alternatives they may have to offer to the closing. The employees might be willing to adjust their wages and benefits, agree to increase productivity levels, or even offer to buy the operation as a way of saving their jobs.

The company is obviously obliged to honor all commitments to employees in the event that closing down is its only option. Wages, benefits, and pensions due have to be paid. But the company could also offer to relocate employees who are willing to move to its operations in other locations at its expense. These employees might also need help with losses due to a devalued real estate market. An employment service could be made available to help employees who can't move to positions in other company locations, and training programs could be set up to help equip them with any skills new jobs might require.

To what degree is this assistance a matter of justice or just a nice gesture? I think it depends on how the implicit long-term contract is interpreted. If employees came on board with the company knowing that it might not be staying around long, it seems clear that they would not have a claim to assistance of this kind in strict justice. But if they were hired and told about all the long-term benefits the company had to offer, encouraged, perhaps, to make a long-term commitment to it, the claim in justice would be stronger. It seems to be a growing practice today, however, for companies to state formally that all benefit packages (except those mandated by law, like vested pensions) may be discontinued at any time. In that case, it would be hard to argue that justice demands special treatment over and above commitments owed to employees strictly for work done or as termination benefits negotiated in a union contract.

In virtue, again, of an implicit long-term contract to the community, the company may have some obligations toward that community before it can pick up stakes and move on:

- It is morally questionable whether a company could move just to avoid paying higher taxes, unless they clearly are the cause of the company's inability to make a reasonable profit. Shareholders are obliged to absorb their fair share of the legitimate costs of sustaining the communities their companies operate in.
- Even if a company were justified in moving out, any tax concessions originally offered to attract it to the community and accepted by the company and, to the extent they can be identified, costs of civic improvements supported by taxes and incurred directly to support the company should be calculated. A reasonable estimate should be made of any shortfalls not covered by the ordinary taxes that were levied on the company over the years and those shortfalls made up.

- Private civic institutions that spent money on improvements indirectly benefiting the company might be entitled to donations in some proportionate amount.

- Independent businesses established to supply a company's operation probably have little or no claim in justice on the company when it shuts down. Their owners had to realize that there was some risk in staking their success on just one or a few large industries. The company might, however, help them out, at least for a short time, by ordering supplies or services from them for its other operations, if it has any.

Again, any moral obligations a company has because it decides to shut down are qualified by its ability to meet them. No one is held to do the impossible.

It's clear that the conclusions I have proposed are based on what the notions of right and justice require relative to closing down a plant. The utilitarian moralist, of course, would have to weigh all the consequences for the company's shareholders, managers, employees, and the community and decide, in each situation, whether the good would outweigh the bad. The cultural relativist would have to rely on the local, state, or federal laws that might govern plant closings, or, in the absence of such laws, find out what society's customs or mores would tolerate.

SUMMARY

We examined, as an example of what a company might owe a community, a case where an automobile manufacturer decided to close down a 30-year operation in a community because, it claimed, the demand for its model built there was down, and the plant was over capacity.

The economic effects on the community threatened to be devastating. Further, critics of the closing saw it as a breach of contract with the community because of all the services the community had provided the company over the years, and because the company, implicitly, at least, had made a long-term commitment to remain in the community.

Another criticism of the closing stressed the fact that the employees had no say in a decision that profoundly affected their lives.

The critics were particularly harsh because they suspected that the company really intended to replace the automobile built in this plant with models made in newly-opened plants in foreign countries.

We looked at the arguments that might be offered for and against the claim that a contract, even though only implicit, was established when the company located its plant in the community.

We saw that the company would likely argue that it had not made any kind of contract with the community. It had to assume that everyone understands how the free-market system works, that buyers and sellers are free to enter and leave the market as they see fit and that no company can operate indefinitely at a loss. Its primary fiduciary responsibility is to its shareholders, and if that responsibility requires shutting down an unprofitable plant, it has a moral obligation to do so. The company might also point out that the community owed it a lot because of the income, taxes, and general level of economic prosperity it had helped generate over the years. It probably had contributed to the community's cultural, social, and religious organizations, and its managers and employees may have assumed leadership roles in them.

Finally, in response to the charge that the employees had no say in the decision to close the plant, the company would likely argue that that decision belonged solely to the company's managers acting in the interests of all the shareholders.

The community's rebuttal would likely include several points: (1) it incurred significant costs to support the company's operations by providing improvements in roads, sewage systems, protective services, and schools; (2) many of the community's businesses were established just to support the plant and its employees; (3) members of the community who had signed on with the company had begun to establish themselves and their families in the community, making long-term commitments to homes, all in the expectation that the company would be there for a long time; (4) the company's managers and employees and their families had benefited from civic, social, and religious organizations the community provided. Surely all these considerations pointed to the existence of an implicit contract with the community.

We examined some practical principles and conclusions we might derive from them that would help determine moral limits to a company's right to close down an operation in a community.

Given a political system that endorses a competitive, free-enterprise economic system, where profit is the *sine qua non* of business, no company can commit itself unreservedly to an indefinite stay in a community. Some circumstances are beyond its control: the material resources it depends on like coal, gas, or oil may be depleted; the market for its products may disappear; it may not be possible to maintain profit levels that will provide equitable and just wages and benefits for its employees; state or local taxes may become confiscatory; government regulations may make it impossible to deliver a product at a price consumers are willing to pay. Employees and the communities where companies locate must understand that they share a risk in an operation that may not turn out to be profitable.

A company that locates operations in a community, especially as a result of political or labor-related incentives offered to it, surely understands that its employees and other members of the community have some legitimate long-term economic expectations from it, that they see the company's operation as a way to exercise their right to access resources. The company knows full well that the community will likely need to improve roads and sewage systems, build schools, and provide other supporting services and institutions. Both the company and the community will benefit from these expenditures, and each has to pay its fair share.

There are some moral limits that may be placed on a company's right to close down an operation in a community.

No company is obliged to remain in operation when it is clear that it cannot continue to make a profit. But as long as it can sustain a reasonable level of profitability, it does have some long-term commitment to remain in a community. It would be morally questionable for a company to relocate just to pay higher dividends to shareholders. Shareholders do have a right to a profit, to access resources for their benefit through their company, but that right is limited by the larger context of social and distributive justice in a free-market economic system.

It would be unjust for a company to move an operation to a foreign country and substitute foreign workers for domestic workers just to maximize shareholder earnings. Foreign workers also have a right to access resources, but not by directly replacing workers in another country. It would also be morally questionable for a company to replace, on a one-to-one basis, its products made in a domestic operation with the same products made in a foreign country if that meant losing domestic jobs.

Employees may not be the owners of a company (except as shareholders), but respect for their dignity as persons demands that they have some say in decisions profoundly affecting their lives. That means they need sufficient advance notion of a plant closing so that they can make plans to cope with it. The company should at least listen to employees' objections, consider the economic needs, and listen to proposed alternatives, for example, for an adjustment in wage and benefit levels in order to keep the plant in operation.

When a plant closes, all of a company's wage, benefit, and pension commitments to employees must be met. Depending on what kinds of long-term promises for continued employment, raises, and pensions were held out by the company, there may be some obligation in justice to relocate employees willing to move to other company operations at company expense, assist these employees with losses caused by a depressed real estate market, and offer retraining and reemployment services for those employees who can't move.

It would be morally questionable for a company to move just to avoid paying higher taxes, unless those taxes made it impossible for the company to earn a decent profit. Shareholders have to do their fair share of sustaining the communities their companies operate in.

Any shortfalls in tax concessions or ordinary taxes levied on the community for civic improvements made in the company's interests should be calculated, if possible, and made up.

Independent businesses established to supply a company's operations probably have no claims against it in justice, although the company might help them out by directing to them business from another one of its operations for a period of time.

The moral conclusions just derived depended on notions of rights and justice, for the most part. The utilitarian moralist would approach this issue by weighing and comparing all the good and bad consequences affecting companies and communities when deciding the morality of closing down a plant. The cultural relativist would be guided by relevant laws, and if there weren't any, by his or her understanding of what society's customs or mores required in this matter.

15

Protecting the Environment

HARMING THE ENVIRONMENT

Most of us are concerned with the actual and potential harmful effects of industrial, manufacturing, and agricultural practices on the environment. The following are some examples:

- Some natural resources (oil, coal, gas) are literally destroyed and lost forever as they are used.
- The destruction of certain resources to provide for human needs may lead to dire consequences for other people. Cutting down the tropical rain forests, for example, provides agricultural opportunities for some people, but that benefit is offset by the claim that these trees absorb huge amounts of carbon dioxide and are very likely a major factor in preventing a possible rise in global atmospheric temperature (the "greenhouse effect") that could partially melt the polar ice caps and flood coastal cities around the world.
- Many chemicals designed to control weeds and pests may be toxic.
- Toxic and other industrial wastes are dumped into streams, rivers, oceans and the air. According to the New Jersey Public Interest Research Group, for instance, "New Jersey's largest industries released over 174 million pounds of hazardous materials into the air, land, and water in 1987" ("Toxic Trends," 1989).

- Fuel and toxic and nuclear wastes are stored in facilities that develop leaks.

- Sulfur emissions from power generating plants contribute to "acid rain" which, according to some experts, contaminates forests, lakes, and streams and destroys aquatic life—often in areas many hundreds of miles away.

- Spills from tankers carrying crude oil contaminate bodies of water, pollute shorelines, and kill wildlife.

There are several issues involved here, and all of them seem to have implications for the moral responsibility of managers. Some resources are completely destroyed and can never be reused by present or later generations. Pollution harms wildlife, plants, natural rock formations, forests, and, of course, human beings. Dirty streams, dumps of every kind, overburden from strip-mining, smog hanging over communities, chemical odors, and dirty smoke from factories and plants in addition to causing harmful effects are unsightly and aesthetically offensive.

Professional ethicists disagree on just what managers are obliged to do to protect the environment. One view is that managers need to develop concern for the environment because that is really concern for the interests of others weighed against one's own interests—like that of making a profit, for example. Another view is that managers need only comply with the environmental laws because that is how, along with decisions made by consumers in the free market, society indicates how much harm to the environment it will tolerate ("Corporate Conscience," 1989).

Some ethicists want to attribute rights to objects in the environment—trees, rock formations, plants, bodies of water and streams, and animals. At very least, they claim, these objects have the right not to be harmed without good reason (Stone, 1983).

Without developing a complex philosophical argument for it here, I will simply state my belief: only actual or potentially self-conscious beings are subjects of rights in the proper sense of that term; therefore, inanimate objects do not have rights, especially the right not to be used up or destroyed for human purposes. Further, I do not think that rights are attributable to animals in the same way they are to human beings, but I do believe they have a right in an extended sense, as sentient beings, to be treated humanely. On my view, then, the only way to establish moral obligations toward the environment is in terms of how harm to the environment affects human beings, with the caveat that animals, among natural objects, do deserve special consideration.[1]

CONSERVATION

Earlier, I attempted to establish the right of human beings to use natural resources from our convictions about the inherent dignity and worth of the human person along with the fact that it's not possible to live decently at some reasonable level of comfort without them. If we are religious believers, we may also hold that God has given us dominion over nature to use as we see fit and that strengthens our claim on it. But how is this right limited? May we use resources for any reason whatsoever? Are we obliged at all to conserve them? If so, for whom? Is it acceptable to fritter away vast amounts of energy on certain kinds of sports, or on developing beautiful lawns and landscapes, or by allowing the unlimited use of private automobiles when public transportation is clearly a more efficient way to move people around? May managers use resources for any enterprise that promises to make a profit?

I think it would be hard to pinpoint any industrial or commercial activity that would be prohibited morally solely because it uses up or even wastes resources (capricious and wantonly cruel treatment of animals is an exception). Not everyone will agree that every use of natural objects contributes to human well-being, but we should at least be cautious before condemning activities which at first blush look like an ill-considered use of resources. They might turn out to be the sole means to someone's livelihood.

I believe that the only use of resources that would be immoral would be one that diverted them from other people's essential needs (including the preservation of natural settings for aesthetic purposes). For example, unlimited use of private automobiles for pleasure in a rich country, whose citizens could afford to bid up the price of oil, might deprive people in poorer nations of the fuel they need for agriculture or basic industrial processes indispensable to maintaining a reasonably decent standard of living for themselves. Justice, then, may require conserving resources to be sure that there will be enough for everyone who needs them for the immediate future, at least until technology provides substitutes.

The aesthetic satisfaction people experience in the simple contemplation of nature's beauty is another reason for practicing conservation. That's why governments set aside land for parks and wildlife refuges and prohibit commercial activity like drilling for oil in certain offshore areas.

These practices are often a source of conflict between environmentalists who support them and companies and workers who want to exploit the resources preserved areas contain. Environmentalists in New Mexico, for example, are fighting a proposal to establish a disposal site for wastes generated by a mine that has provided a living for many people for a good number of years. The workers oppose the environmentalists because without that site, the mine will have to shut down. The workers' plea is very straightforward: not starving to death is more important than preserving birds and clean streams.[2]

Should managers fight environmental proposals that may interfere with a profitable operation? If the situation really boils down to feeding and clothing human beings over preserving resources, the decision ought to favor people's survival needs first. None of these situations is usually that clear-cut, of course, so it appears that managers may legitimately make their cause but not exert undue pressure on politicians and decision makers to decide environmental issues purely on the basis of profit.

The number of people affected in these cases has some bearing here; if just a few jobs, relatively speaking are jeopardized by a conservation project that will ultimately provide aesthetic enjoyment for many thousands of people, the jobs probably should go. But society has an obligation to compensate the people who lose their jobs and help them find work that will maintain their accustomed standard of living.

The significance of the environment's natural beauty for human beings also supports the obligation managers have to avoid damaging it or destroying it just to minimize costs and increase profits. There is, I think, a further obligation to restore it, to the extent possible, when it has been damaged unavoidably by industrial processes. A good example of what I mean is strip-mining, which rips up the ground covering coal deposits close to the surface and leaves a terrible trail of destruction. State governments commonly require coal mining companies to post a bond to insure that areas devastated by strip-mining will be restored to something like their original state.

Are we obliged to conserve resources for future, unborn generations? Without getting involved in a complex philosophical dispute about potential existence, I think we at least have to admit that on the one hand, we do expect these people to show up in our world and have a need for natural resources. Therefore, it makes sense to save some for them. On the other hand, it can be argued that the needs and interests of those now alive seem to have priority, and, as past experience shows, human ingenuity will always find substitutes for those resources we may be in danger of using up. I seem to remember stories that before natural gas was available in commercial quantities, for instance, there was a real fear that whale oil would become scarce and a major source of fuel for lighting people's homes would disappear.

The prudent and conscientious response here, it seems to me, is for managers to conserve resources to the best of their ability in the interests of having enough to go around for the immediate future (fifty years or so, perhaps) with the reasonable expectation that technology will take care of the long-term. That means, for example, designing and manufacturing fuel-efficient vehicles; developing alternate energy sources; recycling metals, tires, plastics and paper; and replanting forests.

DON'T HARM

It is evident that some industrial processes harm people and natural objects. But once we know that a product or process is harmful, how do we go about deciding to eliminate it entirely or reduce its effects? It is safe to say right away, I think, that anytime the cost to do so is insignificant, appropriate action is morally obligatory. The problem is obviously more complex when the consequences of eliminating or reducing these harmful effects will result in major costs or loss of benefits to many people. Even if it's clear that some action should be taken, questions like "how much" and "how soon" immediately arise. The U.S. Government, for instance, recognized that leaded gasoline posed a threat to human health and decided to phase it out over a number of years. But was that enough? Would the costs of immediate conversion to lead-free gasoline have outweighed the harm done to the health of people affected by lead emissions during the phase-out period? Even if we accepted the impossibility of an immediate conversion just in terms of logistics, never mind cost, should we have curtailed any nonessential use of leaded gasoline? Should we, for instance, continue to use it even now for purely recreational purposes like boating and water-skiing knowing full well that we may be contributing to someone else's misery? Is it ever enough to gradually reduce the use of toxic substances when even just one person might die from their effects, or should they be banned outright as soon as they are known to be lethal?

The problem is always stickier when pollution causes death. According to a study reported by *The New York Times* of proposed amendments to the Clean Air Act being considered by Congress,

> . . . reductions in emission of 190 cancer-causing industrial chemicals, Mr. Portney estimates, will probably run $6 billion to $10 billion annually.

But by Government analysis, the risks from these toxic effluents is much smaller than commonly supposed; lives saved will probably not exceed 500 annually. Valuing these lives at $3 million each, the total benefits will fall short of $2 billion.[3]

Does that kind of economic analysis offer a sufficient reason for continuing pollution that will contribute to people's deaths? Isn't there something strange about trying to make this kind of evaluation in terms of dollars and cents, as if money were the ultimate common standard of determining the worth of anything? Aren't apples being compared with oranges?

To further illustrate the moral knot involved here, let's see how a natural-law moralist might approach unraveling it using the principle of double effect on the problem of pollution caused by power plants that use fossil fuels to run their generators. What if their emissions contributed to serious respiratory illness and perhaps death in human beings? Here are the steps this moralist would follow if that were true:

- The act of generating electricity by burning coal is in itself at least morally indifferent; it is not a morally bad kind of act.
- The intent here is to provide human beings with all the "goods" electricity offers, not to cause illness or death.
- Any illness or death that results is not the means by which the good effects are obtained; it is only a foreseeable but indirectly intended and regrettable side effect.

So far so good for the double-effect moralist. The task now is to determine whether there is a due proportion between the good and evil consequences resulting from generating electricity this way. (By the way, the utilitarian moralist must make the same kind of calculation in this case.) The list of good effects seems pretty straightforward; consider just a few:

- hospitals run life-saving devices like respirators, kidney-machines, ICU monitors, and sophisticated operating-room instruments;
- heating systems and air conditioners take care of people's comfort needs;
- the entertainment industry from television to theatre, athletics, and amusement parks couldn't exist without an enormous supply of power available 24 hours a day;

- vast lighting systems on streets and highways help insure people's safety;
- complex communications systems serve the private, public, and commercial needs of millions of people.

Think as well about all the people who make their living from manufacturing, selling, installing, and repairing electrical devices and systems.

On the list of bad effects, we find that these plants may be responsible for the sickness or death of even just a few human beings.

Weighing the good and evil effects against each other in this case is complicated by the difficulty in determining just which plant's emissions are contributing to whose ill-health or death, in what degree, and over what period of time. But I believe that after reflecting on the overall balance between the effects, both the double-effect and utilitarian moralist would conclude that it would not be necessary to shut the plants down immediately. Prudent steps would have to be taken as soon as possible to clean up the emissions, like using particle screening devices or, if feasible, substituting cleaner fuels.

The cultural relativist, of course, would have to follow law or custom in order to decide what to do about this or any pollution problem.

In all cases where pollution is at issue, I think we have to remember that it's just not possible to act on natural resources without causing any harm whatsoever. While it's not necessary to bring down an entire economy in an attempt to avoid harm, we are obliged to minimize it to the extent it is reasonable to do so. What's reasonable will surely depend on the immediacy and extent of the harm, that is over what time period does the pollution affect health or cause death? How many people are involved? What is it doing to natural objects, buildings, and works of art?

Companies are already taking significant steps to conserve and protect the environment from installing scrubbers on smokestacks to recycling krypton gas cathode tubes and using recycled paper in many products. While all of these measures may look like good business practices, it ought to be clear by now that they have a moral dimension as well. They may involve significant costs, although some companies claim that many of them actually reduce manufacturing and operating expenses. Where these measures do increase the cost of making a particular product, it seems that these costs should be internalized by the manufacturer and recouped at least partially in the price of the product. I say partially because customers, the ultimate users of the product, ought to pay some share of environmental protection costs but not necessarily all of them.

Shareholders also have a moral responsibility for the environment, and they may need to bear their fair share of those costs in the form of reduced profits.

Unscrupulous business people might fail to take these measures and attempt to put their competitors at a disadvantage, but if that situation were to become widespread, the government would have to step in and, as a matter of justice, force everyone to follow antipollution procedures.

SUMMARY

Industrial, manufacturing, and agricultural practices use up and destroy natural resources and pollute streams, rivers, oceans, and the air. We explored the moral obligations managers have to control the amount of harm done to the environment.

Some ethicists want to attribute rights to natural objects. I proposed my belief that only persons have rights in the strict sense of the term, and that objects in nature do not have the right not to be used up for human purposes. Concern was expressed for animals, however; as sentient beings they deserve special consideration, and should not be treated capriciously or wantonly.

We are obliged to conserve resources to be sure that there will be enough of them to provide a decent standard of living for all human beings, now and in the future. While the needs of present generations have immediate priority, we may not lose sight of the fact that future generations will come along, and prudence advises us to save sufficient resources for them.

Environmentalists want to preserve the beauty of nature and often fight against the commercial use of resources. Their concern for nature's objects has to be weighed against the need for people to live. Where just a few jobs might be lost to an aesthetic natural preserve, it may be morally acceptable to come down on the side of preservation, but society has an obligation to compensate those who lose their livelihood as a result.

We examined the issue of whether activities that pollute the environment and perhaps harm human beings should always be stopped immediately or phased out over time so as not cause economic harm. Using the case of generating electricity with fossil fuels, it looked like both the natural-law and utilitarian moralists would agree that the consequences of immediately stopping the use of this coal would be worse than the harm it caused, so, for these moralists, at least, not every industrial process has to be halted just because it causes harm—even, unintentionally, to human beings. There is, however, an obligation to reduce this pollution extensively or even eliminate it as soon as technology makes that possible.

We noted that the cultural relativist would be obliged to follow law or custom to resolve any issue involving pollution.

Many industries are involved in taking steps to reduce pollution of the environment. This makes good business sense, but it also has a moral dimension as well. Antipollution techniques are costly, and these costs should be recovered from consumers in the form of higher prices and from shareholders by reducing their profits.

NOTES

1. This view is, of course, "anthropocentric," and is challenged by some philosophers and ecologists. The issue is whether natural objects in the environment have value in their own right so that they are not subject to any and all uses human beings want to make of them. See, for instance, Arne Naess, "The Shallow and the Deep, Long-Range Ecology Movement. A Summary," *Inquiry*, Vol. 16, 1973; or Holmes Rolston III, *Environmental Ethics: Duties to and Values in The Natural World* (Temple University Press, 1987).

2. Johnson, Dirk. "Wildlife vs. Wage Earner Troubles Taos," *The New York Times*, August 14, 1990, pp. A1, A18. Copyright © 1990 by The New York Times Company. Reprinted by permission.

3. Passell, Peter. "What Price Cleaner Air," *The New York Times*, August 15, 1990, p. D2. Copyright © 1990 by The New York Times Company. Reprinted by permission.

16

Summing Up

TWO SETS OF ETHICS?

I don't know whether there is an ethical crisis, in the strict sense of that word, in the American business community; I do know that there is a lot of unethical business activity being reported nearly every day in the media. These accounts of widespread fraud and dishonesty have severely damaged the public reputation of business executives and managers on the whole. Only business people themselves can repair it, and I think they have to start with eliminating the mistaken notion, wherever it exists, that there are two sets of ethics: one for private life and one for business life. The kind of ethical failures I've been talking about in this book are what many people ordinarily would likely see as immoral on their face, such as instances of fraud, deception, lying; deliberately permitting clearly hazardous working conditions; and concealing defects in products. As I asked earlier, why don't the people involved in these situations see them that way? Why would people who wouldn't ordinarily cheat, lie, steal, or knowingly inflict harm on someone think that those kinds of actions might be acceptable as long as they're done on behalf of their companies? What kind of justification could possibly be offered for performing certain actions in the business context that would be seen as immoral in other contexts?

IT'S A DIFFERENT ACT

Maybe what's going on in a lot of cases is that people are just resorting to a moral redescription of their actions.

Take a few of the cases we considered earlier like the one we looked at where a company substituted another company's computer system for its own in order to win a government contract. It was suggested that there really wasn't any lying or deception involved because the managers who decided to make the substitution could argue that they were not necessarily selling a particular hardware configuration but only a capability that their own system, when finally up and running, would furnish as effectively as the one they showed the government's representatives.

Or take the case of a defense contractor who may have understated its original bid ("low-balled") in order to win a contract and then made up any shortfall by the cost-overrun process or by submitting padded vouchers to the government, deliberately inflating its costs. It was suggested that a contractor in this situation might say that it wasn't really deceiving the Government in any way or stealing from it because a close scrutiny of its costs would show that they were right in line with what any other contractor would have incurred, so as long as the product delivered was satisfactory, the government was not being cheated or deceived in any way.

How about a company that submits a bid to a customer that includes equipment not yet commercially available—in direct violation of the customer's bidding specifications? I suggested that the people responsible for the bid might have argued that they were positive they'd have that piece of gear ready when the product was delivered, so they weren't really deceiving anyone.

It seemed perfectly clear when we considered them that these kinds of subterfuges or rationalizations just won't hold water; if, from a moral viewpoint, actions are clearly lying, stealing, or cheating, it's hard to see how they can legitimately be redescribed as something else. Further, there's nothing about the business context that justifies these attempts at redescription. Certainly the customers, other competitors, or government agencies affected would not likely see them that way and would have no trouble claiming that they were lied to or cheated.

IT'S SOMEBODY ELSE'S ACT, BUT I HAD TO DO IT

Another explanation that was offered for acting differently in business situations was the difficulty people may have in deciding whether they are cooperating or not in another person's immoral actions. It's relatively easy to identify the direct moral failures involved in bribery, price-fixing, dumping toxic waste where it will affect a community's water supply, inflating costs, substituting ingredients in a product without telling the public, or tolerating unsafe working practices and environments. But business people may argue that they would not do these things as a result of their own personal decisions; they do them because the company (bosses, top management, the board of directors) wants them done. They may be able to show that their part in what is going on is morally good or indifferent, just "material cooperation," for example,

- lower-level managers only pass on the orders to send out trucks to dump hazardous waste in unprotected locations;
- drivers just drive the trucks and dump the wastes, they don't decide where to dump it;
- managers only provide the professional and technical expertise needed to prepare bids whose questionable content is specified by the company, not by them;
- telephone sales contact people don't like to deceive customers with misleading information, but they don't write the script—the company does;
- owners of employment agencies who honor the directives of clients not to send members of certain minority groups for job interviews are not discriminating; their clients are.

In short, business people are faced with the issue of when material cooperation in somebody else's wrongdoing becomes formal cooperation, so that what they are doing isn't morally right or neutral anymore but an essential contribution to what is morally wrong. And it's easy to see how people may be pressured into formal cooperation when their jobs and their families' welfare are on the line and how they may be tempted to justify themselves on the grounds of coercion. The moral ideal, of course, is to refuse doing whatever our conscience tells us is morally wrong; and only the threat of violence which totally destroys our moral freedom is justified as coercion. In effect, we cannot pass off our moral responsibility to someone else—like the company and claim that it is acting, not us.

WHAT'S GOOD FOR THE COMPANY IS GOOD FOR SOCIETY

Another way people may be trapped into thinking that different moral standards have to apply in the business world is by making a metaphysical mistake, by getting caught up in the size and enormous scope of activity going on in their enterprises. (I have in mind here large corporations more than small businesses or industries.) Business people tend to identify with that scope of activity and with the corporate culture: with the day-to-day social practices among their fellow managers and among bosses and subordinates; with the attitudes toward "outsiders," like customers, competitors, government regulatory agencies, the media, consumer groups; with the ways in which employees are treated in terms of work-performance appraisals, promotions, and salaries. In this corporate culture, many managers find their identities, opportunities for greater prestige and earning power, even their reputation in the community.

In short, I think that many business people come to think of their corporation, a legal fiction, as some kind of entity in its own right, and what appears to foster the well-being of that entity fosters their own and society's well-being. They understand the enormous impact the company's operations have on communities as well as on their own lives. It's easy to see, then, how actions which in nonbusiness contexts might be seen as morally questionable may now be seen as actions that need to be done to achieve the ends which mean so much to the various political and social communities a company serves.

On this view, the moral rules some people use in nonbusiness situations simply can't apply when the stakes for so many people and institutions are so high. People who might otherwise believe that certain actions are wrong in themselves, intrinsically, regardless of their consequences, may think they have to become consequentialists in their business lives. But this ignores all the arguments against pure consequentialism: for example, that it entails that the end may at least sometimes justify the means or that it may violate justice or the personal rights of people.

Some people may become so enamored with the importance of their corporation that they become moral relativists arguing that business should do whatever it has to do to insure profits for its shareholders as long as it stays within the boundaries of society's laws and customs.

We have already seen, however, the difficulties to which this approach to morality leads. If, for instance, laws and ethical customs change, justification for business actions changes. What's banned today may turn out to be acceptable tomorrow, or what is illegal or contrary to ethical custom in our country may not be so in third world countries: for example, dumping toxic wastes near community water supplies; paying the lowest wages possible even if they're not a living wage. Or take the cigarette industry: it would be wrong, on the laws and customs account, for its executives to print a warning on the packages it markets in third world countries that smoking may be hazardous because there may be no laws or social customs compelling it to do so. The warning might lower sales, and that would be contrary to the interests of the shareholders and employees. In effect, it's acceptable to do these kinds of things as long as they aren't illegal or contrary to custom and are in the corporation's interests.

Relativism, however, is still at issue; there is still the case for moral absolutism to be reckoned with, the natural-law moralist's idea that certain actions should never be done. It is possible, for instance, that laws and customs in a society may violate justice. There were no laws or social customs in our own country some 30 years ago forbidding discrimination against women and black people in the workplace (or if there were, they were simply ignored); on a moral relativist's view, it seems that managers would have had to practice discrimination whenever the corporation's interests required it.

In sum, I don't think it can be shown that the business context requires, necessarily, a relativistic or purely consequentialist moral system so that someone who ordinarily follows a nonrelativist or nonconsequentialist system as a matter of conscience in his or her nonbusiness life is bound to change over to this other kind when functioning as a business person.

ARE CORPORATIONS MORAL PERSONS?

Another mistake, in my opinion, is the notion that the corporation can be thought of as a moral person in some way. One philosopher, Peter French, argues that he sees the fundamental criterion for moral personhood to be *intentionality* (I assume he means by that the knowledge and freedom to act) in the corporation's decision-making rules and procedures, and that's enough to make them moral persons (French, 1979). But I'm not sure what that means. Does it mean simply that we can point to corporations like AT&T, GM, Exxon, and Citibank, for instance, and accuse them of moral as well as legal wrong-doing? But we can do that already without needing to first establish them as moral persons because we have this useful linguistic device, a short-cut for attributing actions and responsibility to several individual moral persons: the collective term. That, after all, is what the word "corporation" does for us in our language, it represents a collectivity of shareowners, directors, officers, and employees.

Nor do I see how decision-making rules and procedures, the product of either one person in a corporation or many persons acting together but individually consenting to establish these rules, suddenly generate a moral person, because the only intentionality involved is the intentionality of those individuals making up the rules and procedures in the first place.

Further, if a corporation were a moral person as French holds, would it mean that those executives and managers who act according to its decision-making rules and procedures may transfer their own moral responsibility to the corporation? Could they legitimately say that they don't act; the corporation does? And what if some of the rules and procedures turn out to be immoral either in intent or in consequences? Would that absolve these managers from moral responsibility for them? It can be argued, of course, that no corporation would ever establish those kinds of rules and procedures. Explicitly, perhaps not—but maybe implicitly? Suppose a corporation has as a rule that it will litigate all significant suits against it for product defects as far and as long as the judicial process will allow—with the intent of simply wearing out its opponents. Isn't that an injustice? Further, do informal rules and procedures count? What if it's understood that women are simply not promoted above certain levels of management in a company? Are the executives and managers who follow that rule exempt from moral responsibility for blatant acts of discrimination?

"BUSINESS ETHICS" DON'T EXIST

The final upshot of all this is that the moral redescription of acts, or appeals to undue coercion when questions of material and formal cooperation in somebody else's immorality are at issue, or appeals to consequences for the company's shareholders, employees, customers, and society, or appeals to moral relativism, or establishing corporations as moral persons do not justify business people thinking that the business world requires its own special set of moral principles or that they may pass on their own moral responsibility to a fictitious entity called "the corporation." I think business people have to carry the same conscientiously-held moral principles they use in their private lives into their business lives. This means, in effect, that there is no such thing as business ethics; there is just ethics, moral principles that have to be applied consistently to all situations of human life. I don't deny that it's useful to analyze moral obligations and choices in concrete contexts, like business, nursing, medicine, and law, but it's important to understand that no inherently distinct set of moral principles governs each of these fields.

WHAT SHOULD AN INDIVIDUAL MANAGER DO?

What can an individual business manager do to bring about a better ethical climate in his or her workplace? Some suggestions follow:

- Reflect seriously on the set of moral principles you hold. Are you satisfied with them? Are you a moral absolutist who holds that certain actions are always morally wrong, in themselves, regardless of their consequences? Or are you willing to justify actions solely on the overall good consequences they produce? This reflective effort may mean spending some time reading books or articles on moral theory and on moral problems in the business context. It might even mean attending a seminar or other educational offering on business ethics, especially if it's offered by your company.

- Resolve to apply your conscientiously-held moral principles as consistently as you can in all life situations—including business. Avoid subscribing to the double ethic I just talked about.

- Refuse to do anything you think morally wrong just because your company's supervision asks you to. Confront bosses and subordinates with wrongdoing whenever you think it warranted. Obviously, this requires moral courage.

- If you supervise people, let them know what you expect from them in terms of moral conduct. Do not accept or make excuses for immoral actions your subordinates may do—no matter how much they may argue that it's for the company's good. Most importantly, practice what you preach.

- Resolve to treat all the people you come in contact with in the business world with the dignity and respect they deserve as human beings.

- If you cannot reconcile your conscience with the type of business you are working in or the business actions your company wants you to perform, leave the company.

WHAT SHOULD A CORPORATION DO?

Good ethics in a company start at the top. Here are some suggestions for boards of directors and corporate officers:

- Establish clearly, for your employees, your position on ethical issues in business. Let them know what kind of conduct you expect from them in the context of your operation. While people may differ on the set of moral principles they hold and how they are to be applied, there are certain actions which just about everybody can agree should not be done, especially those that are clearly cases of direct and deliberate harm to people, their property, and the environment. This may sound like simply promulgating the standard type code of ethics which your company may already have, but it goes beyond letting employees know what conduct you want them to avoid only because it may harm the business. It includes how you expect employees to treat customers, fellow employees, the public, suppliers and contractors, and the environment. It will spell out their expected responses to laws which govern your operations and how they are expected to deal with representatives of any government agencies charged with the regulation of your operations.

- Just as you insure that managers are trained to manage by sponsoring training courses, seminars, lectures, etc., you should also provide similar learning experiences in the field of business ethics. This is a good way to be certain that your position and expectations on business ethics are transmitted to your managers and the employee body.

- Establish a formal channel for employees who may be disturbed about certain things going on in the company to express their concerns— without fear of retribution of any kind. Many companies have established departments for employees seeking psychological counseling for alcohol and drug abuse, and visits to these services are kept totally confidential. If employees know they have a place to carry their legitimate complaints and that their anonymity will be respected, it's likely that external whistle-blowing will never or rarely be needed in a company.

- Practice what you preach. That's one of the best ways to let people know what you expect of them. Most importantly, do not send ambiguous messages to your managers and employees either in your actions or verbal and written communications about how they are to act in situations requiring good moral as well as good business judgment. Apply to yourselves the suggestions I offered earlier for individual business managers who want to improve the moral climate of their workplaces.

SUMMARY

I believe that many people would think that the kinds of ethical failures we've discussed in this book are immoral on their face, apparent instances of fraud, deception, and lying or directly harming people. Why didn't the people who were involved in these situations see them as possible moral failures? What justifications could they offer for performing actions in the business context that they might see as immoral in other contexts? In effect, do some business people think there are two sets of ethics: one for their business lives and one for their private lives?

We looked at ways people might try to get themselves off the moral hook.

It was suggested that some actions might be redescribed so that they would not really be morally wrong. Some of the cases we analyzed in earlier chapters were used as examples:

- In the action where a computer company substituted another company's system for its own and told its client that the substitute was its own system looked like a lie, someone might try to argue that it wasn't a hardware configuration that was being shown but only a capability; therefore, the company did not lie to its customer.

- Deliberately understating costs in bids for Government contracts or overbilling the Government might be justified using the rationale that the final costs billed would be right in line with what other contractors would have incurred had they gotten the bids, so the Government was not really being cheated.

- Including equipment not commercially available in a bid in direct violation of the client's bidding specifications could be justified on the presumption that it would be available later on in time to meet the contract deadlines.

I argued that these rationalizations do not work, that when actions would clearly be seen as instances of lying or cheating or deliberately harming people, as immoral, in nonbusiness contexts, there's nothing about the business setting that allows them to be redescribed as something else.

Another explanation for acting differently in business situations is that what is being done is done on the initiative or even orders of the company (bosses, top management), and that one's own action is in itself morally acceptable. A manager just dispatches the trucks dumping toxic waste in unprotected locations but doesn't make the decision to dump there; the people driving the trucks hauling this waste just drive the trucks and don't decide where to dump their loads; managers just provide the professional expertise needed for bids whose morally questionable content is really specified by somebody else in the company; telephone sales people make misleading pitches from scripts not made by them but by higher-ups in management; an employment agency that honors a client's request not to send members of certain minorities for job interviews is not discriminating, the client is.

The issue here is to determine when material cooperation is legitimately distinguishable from formal cooperation in someone else's immoral act.

Coercion is sometimes offered by managers as a reason for doing things for the company that they would not do in their private lives, but it seems that only the threat of violence that would destroy a person's freedom is a sufficient excuse for doing something he or she thinks is morally wrong.

The defense, then, that "I'm not acting; the company is" often rests on shaky moral premises.

Some managers get so caught up in the size and scope of their company's operations and the impact these operations have on society that for them, the company's interests become the interests of everybody in the communities it serves. Managers also become so involved with their company's corporate culture, in their day-to-day interactions with other managers, bosses, employees, and the public that they find their own identities, earning power, and reputations in the company, and they may come to think of their company as an entity in its own right. The stakes, then, for this entity and the communities affected by it are seen to be so high that the moral rules that apply to individuals can't be applied to its operations. Managers, for instance, whose moral orientation is ordinarily nonconsequentialist might think they have to become consequentialists in their companies' interests.

Managers may also become moral relativists who believe that whatever a business does is morally sound as long as it stays within the bounds of society's laws and customs. This approach, as we have seen, has its own difficulties: what's morally acceptable today may change tomorrow if laws or customs change. What's considered harmful to people or the environment and therefore forbidden in economically advanced countries may be lawful or acceptable in a third-world country. This approach, of course, runs headlong into the moral absolutist's position that certain actions should never be done. There is nothing, however, about the business context in itself that justifies moral relativism in business situations.

We examined Peter French's contention that corporations may be considered moral as well as legal persons because their decision-making rules and procedures provide the intentionality, the knowledge and freedom required to be a moral person. I argued that this is a mistake. The term "corporation" serves us as a linguistic device; it allows us to refer collectively to the actions of many different people. In the final analysis, however, only individual intentionality is involved. Even when people act together, each one individually consents to the action seen as a product of the group's efforts: such as when setting up corporate policies and procedures.

The problem I saw with thinking about the corporation as a moral person was that some managers might be tempted to think that as long as they follow their company's decision-making rules and procedures, they may transfer their individual moral responsibility to the company—even if some of the rules and procedures (even informal ones) turn out to be immoral in intent or purpose.

I concluded that there is no such thing as business ethics, that there are just ethics, moral principles that should be applied consistently to all life's situations whether in business, nursing, medicine or law.

I proposed some things managers might do to help improve the moral climate of their companies:

- Reflect conscientiously on the set of moral principles you hold and satisfy yourself that you want to continue to hold them or change to another set. It may be necessary to do some reading or formal or informal study in the field of ethics to accomplish this. In any case, apply your principles consistently in all life situations.
- Don't act in ways you think are morally wrong just because your company's supervisors ask you to. Confront bosses and subordinates with wrongdoing whenever you think it's warranted.
- If you supervise people, let them know what you expect by way of moral conduct.
- Treat all the people you come in contact with in your business dealings with the respect they deserve as human beings.
- If you can't reconcile your conscience with the kinds of actions your business requires of you, resign and work somewhere else.
- Practice what you preach.

I also proposed some things boards of directors and corporate officers might do to establish a sound moral climate in their enterprises:

- Clearly set out your position on ethical issues in business. Let your managers and employees know what conduct you expect from them in the context of your operation. People will differ on the source of their moral principles and, possibly, on what they judge morally right or wrong, but there are a number of actions everybody will agree should be avoided because of the harm they do to people, property, or the environment.

- Just as you provide seminars and training courses designed to help run the company more effectively and profitably, consider adding seminars and training courses on business ethics to your company training programs. That's a first-rate way of passing on to your employees the kind of business conduct you expect from them.

- Establish a formal channel for employees to talk about and get advice on situations in the company that are causing them moral concern.

- Practice what you preach.

Appendix: Utilitarianism, Natural Law, and Cultural Moral Relativism—An Expanded Version

In this appendix, I want to explore in more detail what grounds of moral obligation two moral theories, utilitarianism and the Thomistic version of natural law, offer, and what cultural moral relativism holds about the possibility of determining any universal standard of morality.

CULTURAL MORAL RELATIVISM

One approach to moral decision making is to claim that there is no one moral standard, that there is no objective measure of right or wrong. All morality is relative to the customs, mores, practices, or laws of a particular culture or society. People who do business in the international market often resort to this view when, for example, they argue that the morality of paying a bribe to government officials in a foreign country in order to do business there depends solely on whether or not the people in the country consider bribery immoral.

Every society, past and present, is characterized by a moral code of some kind. Cultural anthropologists and sociologists offer us evidence that these codes have differed and do differ among societies and that many of the practices regarded as immoral by one society are often regarded as quite acceptable by others. Some cultures have been known to kill female babies in order to preserve a balanced female-to-male ratio in the population. Other cultures see this as a heinous crime. People identified as witches were burned at the stake at one period of history; no enlightened society would permit this today. Sexual customs like incest and polygamy have been accepted in some cultures but outlawed in others. Attitudes toward what parts of the human body may be uncovered in public differ among societies. Cannibalism, torture, and inhumane methods of punishment and execution have been sanctioned in various cultures; other cultures find these practices repulsive. Some ancient societies ate their dead; others burned theirs. Each would be appalled at the other's practice. Slavery was considered morally legitimate in the American South; the North considered it immoral, and many Northerners were ready to die to get rid of it.

These differences in moral practices among societies are commonly referred to as cultural relativism. When a moral theorist argues that moral obligation is located in these practices, that is that a member of a society is held bound to observe what they command and forbid, that moralist is arguing for normative relativism. The challenge for this view of morality is to show how that obligation arises, why cultural relativism is normative.

One American sociologist and philosopher, William Graham Sumner (1840–1910) developed an extensive theoretical treatment of cultural moral relativism. He argued that groups of primitive people, adapting to interests defined by the concrete circumstances of their daily existence (especially experiences involving pleasure and pain) developed practices, folkways. These folkways, handed down as tradition in a culture, do not stem from reason. People conform to them, they are binding, because their ancestors, the "ghosts," have handed them down through the generations. "The notion of right is in the folkways" (Sumner, 1979). When the earliest generations of human beings understood, however dimly, that the folkways were conducive to welfare, they became mores. Mores, then for Sumner, are simply "historical, institutional, and empirical" (Sumner). They are not developed from some external standard, they are not the product of reason, and they will vary from culture to culture. But they are seen as binding on the members of these cultures, at least in the sense that the members consistently observe what the mores prescribe and forbid.

Note that underlying Sumner's explanation of the transition from folkways to mores is the notion of welfare. Apparently, this means that these practices are perceived, again, however dimly, as good, valuable, for a people, that they contribute to its well-being. Further, some of the mores become laws when they are reflected on and turned into rational, practical measures (Sumner). But even then they are not dependent on some external standard of morality, they are relative to that particular society's reflections and perceptions of what is practical.

A theory that sees moral obligation solely as a product of cultural relativism appears to make moral decision-making simple. To know what to do or refrain from in any given situation, a person just follows the customs, mores, practices or laws of the culture or society he or she happens to be in at the time. It could be especially appealing to business people who might think it easier to operate in a society where bribery and kick-backs to government officials seem to be the way of life, or where there are no customs or laws against pollution, or no customs or laws that require insuring safe conditions in the workplace, labeling products that might be dangerous to people's health, or paying a minimum wage. Milton Friedman, a contemporary economist, seems to argue this way. For Friedman, corporate executives have just one fiduciary responsibility: to make as much money for stockholders as they can while "conforming to the basic rules of the society, both those embodied in law and those embodied in ethical custom" (Friedman, 1970). Of course, the other side of the coin is that local customs and laws may be so restrictive that they might make doing business in a particular society impractical or even impossible.

This view of morality is powerfully persuasive to many people, but it does run into some serious theoretical difficulties that challenge its soundness.

Let's start first with the argument cultural moral relativists might offer that given the great variety in human moral codes, both past and present, we have to conclude that a standard of morality that could guide all human beings everywhere at all times in all situations can't possibly exist. But this reasoning is logically fallacious because it moves from what is, the fact of variety in moral practices, to the conclusion that a universal moral standard is impossible. In other words, the argument says that because people behave differently, no moral standard exists. But simple differences in moral behavior do not, by themselves, logically entail a true conclusion about the existence or nonexistence of a moral standard. This is like saying that children playing sandlot baseball often make up different rules for their particular games, and that fact must mean that a standard set of rules for playing the game can't exist.

Consider as well that while concrete cultural practices do differ, there do seem to be common values among all societies. Murder, if accepted, would threaten the very existence of the society, and no culture seems to find it acceptable. The interactions a society's members need for their everyday living would be impossible if breaking promises and lying were acceptable. Every society seems to have sexual mores whose underlying thrust is to protect the community, however they may differ from other communities' sexual practices. So, while there may appear to be clear differences in moral codes among societies, these may really be superficial and, if examined more closely, seen to rest on some common, universal, moral foundations.

Another theoretical difficulty for moral relativism is that in the absence of a universal moral standard, there is no way of ever judging that certain moral practices are better than others, that one society is more moral than another. A society that approved polygamy, infanticide, slavery, and genocide, for instance, could be judged no worse, morally speaking, than one that prohibited these practices. People in a given society might never justify making it "better" by way of deep philosophical reflection and moral argument.

Then there's the problem of deciding just what a particular culture is, just what group of people a society includes. It's probably a simple matter to define a group in primitive conditions where it's evident that a particular set of people are a separate "tribe" with their own customs and traditions. But it is obviously more difficult in complex societies. In the United States, for example, certain subgroups may believe that polygamy or homosexuality is morally acceptable or may adopt religious practices or experiences like snake-handling or smoking peyote. People in the larger community, however, may find these customs objectionable. How does one determine which group's customs or mores should be followed? The old adage, "when in Rome, do as the Romans" may be difficult to follow if one cannot figure out what and whom "Rome" includes.

Or, take the difference between the laws established by a community and its customs. Which has preference, morally speaking? The law may prohibit speeding over 55 m.p.h. but the majority of the people in the community may "customarily" ignore it and average 65 m.p.h. Adultery may be illegal but that law may never be enforced because the "custom" in the community may be for everyone to mind his or her own business. There may be laws against bribing government officials but it may be that "everybody does it." In effect, do the laws or its "customary" practices define the mores of the community? Which prevail as the moral rules to be followed?

Finally, where does the obligation to obey the mores or laws of a society come from? Why do its members observe them? Are they simply afraid of punishment or social ostracism? If so, do people only obey when there's a chance of being caught in a violation? Or do they obey from some deep feeling of duty to their ancestral traditions or their culture's "way of life"? If they obey because they want to promote their community's welfare, it seems that they are relying on a standard of some kind after all, and are not really relativists.

In the analysis of moral problems, I assume that the cultural moral relativist acknowledges an obligation to obey whatever mores or laws a society's members embrace.

MORAL ABSOLUTISM

The other approach to moral decision-making proposes one universal standard for determining whether a particular action is morally right or wrong, a standard that applies to everyone, everywhere, at any time and, as a result, is "absolute." We will look now at two theories that are examples of moral absolutism: utilitarianism and the Thomistic version of natural law.

UTILITARIANISM

Utilitarianism appeals to the principle of utility, which rests fundamentally on the idea that all human beings (and, for some philosophers, all "sentient" beings) want to be happy. Jeremy Bentham (1748–1832), the founder of modern utilitarianism, started with the idea that pleasure and pain are our two ruling masters and that all moral questions have to be resolved in the light of that truth. A morally right action promotes a person's or community's interest by adding to the sum total of its pleasure (which for Bentham was a synonym for happiness) and is morally wrong when it diminishes that pleasure. He provided a set of guidelines for determining the value of any pleasure or pain, along with a sort of "hedonic calculus" according to which an action is judged morally right to the extent that it produces a net balance of pleasure over pain.

John Stuart Mill (1806–1873), a disciple of Bentham, accepted the "pleasure" approach of Bentham's utilitarianism but refined it by rejecting Bentham's claim that all pleasures are qualitatively the same and differ only in quantity. Mill distinguished between higher and lower pleasures, arguing in a famous quotation that "it is better to be a human being dissatisfied than a pig satisfied; better to be Socrates dissatisfied than a fool satisfied."

Since happiness is a result of the effect events have on people, the commonly accepted way of expressing the fundamental thrust of utilitarian moral theory is that the action that generates the most good consequences, states of affairs, on the whole in a situation, or, as it is often stated, the greatest good for the greatest number, is morally right and ought to be performed. An action that produces more bad than good consequences on the whole is morally wrong and must be avoided.

Utilitarian moralists distinguish between "act" and "rule" utilitarianism depending on whether they hold that the good and bad consequences of each individual act make it right or wrong or whether the consequences of general rules of conduct are what should count. But both versions rely fundamentally on the idea that only consequences determine whether an act is right or wrong.

Interestingly, some moralists consider utilitarianism to be a relativist theory "yielding different results under different conditions" (Abelson & Friquegnon, 1987) while others (e.g., Hospers, 1972) classify it as absolutist because it appeals to a universal standard of right action— the most good on the whole. One explanation for this difference might lie in what it means to describe an action. Take the act of murder. If its essential description is limited to "intentionally and directly taking the life of an innocent person," some moral absolutists (for example, Thomistic natural-law moralists) would see it as wrong in itself, absolutely, for everybody, everywhere, at all times. Others might see its description as incomplete until all its attendant circumstances and consequences are included, and in that sense, its rightness or wrongness is relative to circumstances and consequences. Utilitarianism could be seen as falling into this category. Still other moralists might argue that the act cannot be described for purposes of making a moral judgment about it until it is described completely, with all attendant consequences, and only then is it judged according to one universal moral standard: for the utilitarian, the good on the whole, the most good for the most people. On this account, utilitarianism would be an absolutist theory.

Utilitarians hold that in making moral judgments, the good of everyone involved in a particular situation has to be weighed. Each person is equal to every other person. The advantages the action will produce for the person performing it don't count for any more than the advantages or disadvantages for everybody else whom it may affect.

A good illustration of the act-utilitarian approach to moral decision making is President Harry Truman's decision to end World War II in 1945 by dropping atomic bombs on Hiroshima and Nagasaki, Japan.

The President believed he could not accept the estimated loss of millions of American and Japanese lives if Japan had to be invaded to force its surrender, so he elected to kill a significant but by far smaller number of Japanese civilians (most of whom, I think, had to be considered innocent as far as their direct contribution to the Japanese war effort was concerned) in order to make their leaders understand the terrible destructive power of America's new weapon and persuade them to surrender immediately. In effect, Truman decided to perform the action he thought would result in the most good consequences for the most people.

Business people, oriented as they are toward goals and objectives, might find utilitarianism attractive as a moral strategy for their business dealings. It does seem to square with the way we try to deal with life's ordinary dilemmas. We constantly balance the effects of our actions on our life situations: on our families, friends, health, or bank accounts. It seems logical to use the same approach to business situations that are morally ambiguous. Since it is relatively easy to see how a business' or corporation's financial health affects its stockholders, employees, and members of local and national communities, it may look like profit is a reasonable way to measure their well-being. It may seem right to perform an action that appears immoral on its face like lying, cheating, bribing, stealing, or damaging someone's health or property because of the good it will do by its direct contribution to the company's bottom line and, indirectly, to the people a profitable company supports. But business managers may want to consider some of the criticism to which utilitarianism has been subjected and the difficulties involved in applying it to concrete situations.

First of all, how do we go about assessing the extent of the consequences an action may have? How far into the future can or should consequences be projected? How do we know when the interests of everyone concerned have been considered? As business people, do we consider the effects of business decisions on just our immediate or national communities or do we have to consider the international community as well? The utilitarian moral theorist can always point out, of course, that these difficulties are due to the fact that human beings are limited in their ability to foresee and comprehend all the implications of our actions, not to the basic thrust of utilitarianism. True enough. But there are other features of the theory that at least ought to make us pause before we give it our whole-hearted endorsement.

Wouldn't it, for instance, allow the end to justify the means in certain situations? Is there any action, no matter how unspeakable it may seem in itself, that could not be justified as long as a net good state of affairs resulted from it? Could a case often be made, on the basis of consequences, for cheating or lying to customers, or for ignoring the conditions of a contract or for seriously harming the environment? What happens to certain rights we believe individuals have, to life and liberty, for example, (two rights considered "unalienable" for Americans), to a family, privacy, property, or freedom from unjust harassment by governments or individuals? Couldn't any of these be sacrificed if the greater good on the whole required it? If punishing innocent people would put a stop to a wave of serious crime, wouldn't that be the right thing to do, provided the interests of enough other people were at stake? Think of how Japanese–Americans were interned in camps at the start of World War II, allegedly out of fear that some of them might be Japanese agents.

Finally, the intention a person has in mind when acting is not important, morally speaking, to utilitarians; as long as an action brings about a net good state of affairs, it is all right to do it, it "ought" to be done. A person might be acting from the worst motives, but they have no moral significance in themselves; only consequences count. The idea of moral character is probably meaningful for the utilitarian only to the extent that it indicates a person's disposition or lack of it toward producing good states of affairs on the whole. It is true that the effect an action may have on the character of the person doing it may well be one of the consequences to be weighed in deciding what to do, but it doesn't carry any special moral weight over and above that.

THOMISTIC NATURAL LAW

A theory that differs significantly from utilitarianism uses the idea of human nature to establish the grounds of moral obligation. One version of this theory which has had a profound influence on Western culture was initiated by St. Thomas Aquinas (c. 1225–1274) who fused Aristotle's naturalism with Christian theology. The philosophical thinking used to develop this version of natural-law morality has been and still is a significant basis for the official moral teaching of the Catholic Church.

Aquinas believed that morality had to begin with an understanding of human nature. He argued that we humans are essentially goal–driven, inclined toward the good, toward happiness, as demonstrated by our instincts for self-preservation and preserving the human species, for discovering the truth, and for living in association with others, in society. He was convinced that from a purely natural standpoint, reason, reflecting on the inclinations profoundly rooted in our human nature, is capable of judging how they are to be satisfied so that they will promote our complete well-being, our perfection. For Aquinas, reason functions as a lawgiver, commanding that actions which do in fact promote our good are morally right and should be done, but any that diminish it in a significant way are morally wrong and must not be done. Moreover, Aquinas claimed that all of our goal–seeking is subordinated to one final end: eternal happiness which consists of seeing God face-to-face. Finally, since human nature is God's creation, reason reflects God's law for all human beings: the eternal law. As a result, reason only commands what God wants us to do and what He wants us to avoid given our human nature as He has created it. The ultimate source of moral obligation, then, is what God commands, and what He commands can be known by human reason reflecting on human nature.

Consequences, while often important for this theory in deciding what does or does not contribute to the well-being and perfection of the human person, are not how we ultimately judge whether an action is morally right or wrong. An act that always produces bad effects at all times and in all circumstances would be "unnatural" if done generally because it violates nature's essential tendency toward preserving itself. The effects, then, by themselves, don't make the action bad or wrong; they show that the act is unnatural, and that's what makes it wrong (Cronin, 1909), (Gonsalves, 1981).

Unlike utilitarianism, this theory argues for the absolute inviolability of human rights in certain circumstances and provides a role for intention and moral character in deciding what is right or wrong. It holds, for example, that murder, the direct, intentional, killing of an innocent person, as a means to avert evil consequences can never be justified because it is intrinsically wrong; it always strikes at the most basic of human drives: staying alive. In the example cited earlier, President Truman's decision to kill innocent Japanese as a means to force their leaders to surrender unconditionally was not morally legitimate even though it may have saved millions of lives.

Natural-law moralists hold that many actions are morally wrong in themselves because they violate human nature in fundamental ways and, as a result, may never be done, no matter how many good consequences they might produce. Examples include murder, suicide, lying, and deceit in all forms (defined here as withholding the truth from someone who has a right to it), stealing (taking, without permission, what rightfully belongs to someone else), and rape.

Many actions are, of course, morally good in themselves or at least they are morally indifferent, like helping the poor and needy, worshipping God, marital sex, bearing and rearing children, intellectual and aesthetic pursuits, sports, and the exchange of goods and services in the market-place—anything, in effect, that is seen to contribute to the development and perfection of human beings. Intention and other circumstances, however, may make even these actions wrong. If, for example, I give someone a helping hand as part of a scheme to defraud or seduce her, my intention vitiates my act. Sexual intercourse is good in itself, but sex with someone else's partner is adultery. An important feature of this theory is that intention may make an action wrong, but it can never make an action that is intrinsically wrong morally right. I may not murder someone, even if my intention is to save the lives of other people.

It follows, then, that for this theory, the end never justifies the means. Actions considered wrong in themselves may never be done—no matter what good consequences they might produce. This moral stricture poses a problem for many people, because they often find themselves in situations where they want to bring about some good state of affairs but realize that evil as well as good effects will result from their action. It seems that if they were to follow the rules laid down by this theory, they could not prevent events from occurring that their moral instincts tell them should never be allowed to happen. Many people, for example, cannot accept the idea that President Truman's decision to bomb Hiroshima and Nagasaki could possibly be considered immoral, given the enormous number of human lives at stake. Other situations come to mind: what do we do about saving the woman whose ectopic pregnancy is threatening her life? What about cases of self-defense (of which war is an instance) when we know that the deaths of others may unavoidably result from our actions? What about preserving the existence of a corporation on which thousands of people may depend for their livelihood if the only means to save it seem to be deceit or a coverup or bribery or harm to someone else's life or property?

Moralists in the tradition of Aquinas are well aware that some actions bring about good effects accompanied, necessarily, by evil effects. Their solution to this dilemma is the principle of double effect that permits such actions when their evil effects are unintended and only tolerated. This principle specifies the following:

1. The action to be performed may not be morally wrong in itself; for example, it may not be an instance of murder, suicide, theft, or lying,

even though doing it might result in good effects that appear to outweigh its evil effects.

2. The agent's intention must be morally good. He or she must intend only the good effect and merely "tolerate" the evil effect.

3. The evil effect may not be the means by which the good effect is achieved because it would mean that the agent directly intended evil. The end *never* justifies the means.

4. There must be a due proportion between the good and evil effects.

The common examples will illustrate how the principle is supposed to work. The first is self-defense, where my defensive action (stopping an unjust attack on my life) may also result in the death of the attacker. The intention here is to stop the attack, not kill the attacker—whose death I must not intend. The attacker's death is not the means by which my life is saved; stopping the attack is. There is a due proportion between the good and evil effects: my life is at least equal in value to the attacker's.

The second example of the principle's correct use is the situation where a pain-killing drug is given to a person suffering intense, unendurable pain, say from cancer. A physician may prescribe and a nurse administer doses that are large enough to ease the sufferer's pain but will also hasten his or her death. The action of relieving pain is morally legitimate in itself; the death of the sufferer is not the means by which the pain is relieved; the sufferer's death is not, we assume, intended, and there is a reasonable proportion between alleviating unbearable pain and shortening a sufferer's life.

If any of these rules is violated, if, for instance, the evil effect is directly intended by the agent or the evil effects outweigh the good effects, the action is morally wrong and may not be done.

Note the difference here from utilitarian moral theory: for the utilitarian, the act is not judged morally right or wrong until the consequences are weighed, so the restriction of not committing an act morally wrong in itself is meaningless. Also meaningless is the condition that the agent may not intend the evil effect—since the utilitarian doesn't consider intention morally relevant in itself. (The fact that the agent intends evil might, because of its effect on his or her character, be one of the bad consequences to be considered in the utilitarian calculus.)

Note as well that the rule about due proportion between the good and evil effects is similar to the utilitarian calculus and is subject to all the same difficulties like determining who and what are affected by an action's effects and how far into the future its effects extend.

Applying this principle can be just as difficult as applying the utilitarian principle.

DIFFERENT MORAL THEORIES MAY YIELD
DIFFERENT MORAL PRINCIPLES

It should be evident from the consideration of just these two moral theories and cultural moral relativism that different principles for guiding ethical decision making may be derived from different grounds of moral obligation. That is why it's important for people who want to feel comfortable, ethically speaking, with their business decisions need to reflect conscientiously on the theoretical basis for the set of moral principles and beliefs they hold. They need to decide whether they are satisfied that it is sound or whether they need to adopt another set derived from a more convincing moral theory.

SUMMARY

To better understand and resolve moral conflicts we encounter in our business lives, we need to reflect, in the light of moral theory, on the moral beliefs we hold.

A moral theory provides reasons, grounds for determining whether an action is morally right or wrong. According to some theories, there is one universal moral standard for everyone (moral absolutism) or there is no such standard (moral relativism). Some moralists hold that there are certain actions wrong in themselves, such as murder, suicide, and lying, and believe that no reason ever justifies performing them. Others believe that no action can be judged immoral in itself; circumstances and social conditions will play the decisive role in determining whether or not a given action is wrong.

Cultural moral relativism argues that moral obligation lies solely in the customs, mores, or laws of a culture or society. To be moral, just obey society's accepted practices. But cultural moral relativism has its own weaknesses. Its proponents commit a logical fallacy when they argue from the fact of different cultural practices to the conclusion that no universal moral standard is possible. This theory about morality does not provide a way to judge one society better than another or to argue from deep philosophical reflection that a particular society could be made morally "better." It may also fail to recognize that there may really be a universal moral foundation disguised by cultural differences. Finally, it is not always easy to determine where a particular culture or society begins and ends, where one clear set of practices are accepted by a given population.

We saw that utilitarianism looks to overall consequences on the whole as the sole criterion for deciding whether an action is right. Although this theory may have a strong attraction for practical–minded business people, it has some shortcomings. It seems, for example, that producing overall good consequences in certain circumstances might infringe on the rights of individuals or override considerations of justice. The end might justify the means, however heinous they may seem.

Thomistic natural-law theory looks to human nature, its intellectual, physical, and psychological characteristics as the measure of morality. An action that promotes the human person's well-being is morally right; one that detracts from it is morally wrong. For Aquinas, reason, reflecting on human nature, legislates, promulgates the dos and don'ts of the natural law and, in so doing, reflects what the eternal law of God who created human nature wants for that nature. Consequences are useful in deciding whether a particular action is morally right or wrong, but they are not the ultimate criterion for that judgment.

One problem this theory poses for some people is that it regards certain actions as intrinsically wrong (murder, suicide, and lying), and never allows them—even if they would produce significant good consequences overall. This difficulty is offset somewhat by the theory's use of the double-effect principle under which a person may directly produce a good effect even though it is necessarily accompanied by an evil effect. This is morally acceptable as long as the act is good or morally indifferent in itself, the agent doesn't intend the evil effect or use it as the *means* to achieve the good effect, and there is a due proportion between the two effects.

An examination of these approaches to morality clearly shows that different theories may generate different principles for judging actions morally right or wrong. Business people need to reflect on their own principles and determine whether they are comfortable with them or whether they need to convert to some other theory's principles.

References

Abelson, R., & Friquegnon, M. (Eds.). (1987). *Ethics for modern life* (3rd ed.). New York: St. Martin's Press, p. 13.

Andrews, E. (1989, July 31). F.D.A. inquiry on generic drugs focuses on switch of ingredients. *The New York Times*, A1, A10.

Arvanites, D., & Ward, B. (1988). Employment at will: a social concept in decline. *Journal of the Proceedings of the Eastern Academy of Management*, pp. 91-93.

Berg, E. (1991, January 10). U.S. is said to pursue pension case. *The New York Times*, p. D7.

Blumenthal, W. (1977, January 9). Business morality has not deteriorated—society has changed. *The New York Times*, Sec. 4, p. 9.

Brophy, B. (1985, February 27). Woman fired over dating gets $300,000 in damages. *USA Today*.

Clymer, A. (1985, June 9). Low marks for executive honesty. *The New York Times*, Sec. 3., p. 1.

Coke exec will testify in price fix. (1987, June 25). *New York Post*, p. 41.

Corporate conscience, money and motorcars. (1989). *Business Ethics Report*, pp. 2–5. Waltham: Bentley College, Center for Business Ethics.

Cronin, M. (1909). *The science of ethics* (Vol. 1). New York: Benziger Brothers, pp. 135–142.

DeGeorge, G. (1987, April). Picking up the pieces at Paradyne. *Business Week*, p. 102.

DeGeorge, R. (1990). *Business ethics* (3rd ed.). New York: Macmillan, pp. 311,

319–321.

Dewey, J. & Tufts, J. (1932). *Ethics* (Rev. ed.). New York: Henry Holt, p. 173.

Dworkin, R. (1981). What is equality? Part II: equality of resources. *Philosophy and Public Affairs, 10*, 283–345.

Dworkin, R. (1983, February). Why liberals should believe in equality. *New York Review of Books, 30*, pp. 32–34.

Etzioni, A. (1985, November 15). Shady corporate practices. *The New York Times*, p. A35.

French, P. (1979). The corporation as a moral person. *American Philosophical Quarterly, 16*, pp. 207–215.

Friedman, M. (1970, September). The social responsibility of business is to increase its profits. *The New York Times Magazine*, pp. 33, 122–126.

47 box executives draw jail and fines for rigging prices. (1976, December 1). *The New York Times*, pp. A1, D9.

Gonsalves, M. (1981). *Fagothey's right and reason* (Rev. ed.). St. Louis: C. V. Mosby, pp. 174–185.

Guilty plea by ex-officer of Beech–Nut. (1989, November 14). *The New York Times*, pp. D1, D4.

Gruson, L. (1986, July 16). Litton unit to pay $15 million to U.S. *The New York Times*, pp. A1, D4.

Hospers, J. (1972). *Human conduct*. New York: Harcourt Brace Jovanovich, p. 36.

Jackall, R. (1988). *Moral mazes*. New York: Oxford University Press, p. 109.

Johnson, D. (1990, August 14). Wildlife vs. wage earner troubles Taos. *The New York Times*, pp. A1, A18.

Lev, M. (1990, July 31). Guilty plea on billing by Ametek. *The New York Times*, p. D4.

Maguire, D. (1977, October). Quotas: unequal but fair. *Commonweal, CIV*, 647–652.

Noonan, J. (1984). *Bribes*. New York: Macmillan, p. 703.

O'Connell, F. (1962). *Outlines of moral theology* (2nd ed.). Milwaukee: Bruce, p. 118.

Passell, P. (1990, August 15). What price cleaner air? *The New York Times*, p. D2.

Peabody Coal Co. pleads guilty in miner's death. (1986, June 4). *The New York Times*, p. A15.

Pollack, A. (1983, March 31). Issue of deceit in electronics. *The New York Times*, p. D2.

Roche, J. (1971, May). The competitive system, to work, to preserve, and to protect. *Vital Speeches of the Day*, p. 445.

Schanberg, S. (1985, May 14). Color accountability gray. *The New York Times*, p. A27.

Schiller, Z. (1988, October). Ashland just can't seem to leave its checkered past behind. *Business Week*, pp. 122–126.

Snel, A. (April, 1985). A manager who blew the whistle. *The Progressive*, p. 17.

St. Thomas Aquinas. (1952). *Summa Theologiae* (II–II, q. 61, a.1. ad. 3). Madrid: Biblioteca De Autores Cristianos.

Stone, C. (1983). Should trees have legal standing?—Toward legal rights for natural objects. Edited by M. Snoeyenbos, R. Almeder, & J. Humber. *Business ethics*. Buffalo: Prometheus Books.

Sullivan, J. (1989, August 29). New Jersey car insurers profited on waste. *The New York Times*, p. 34.

Sumner, W. (1979). *Folkways and Mores*. Edited by E. Sagarin. New York: Schocken Books, pp. 28, 29, 56.

They whistled and won. (1988, June). *Time, 131* (26), p. 50.

Tomasko, R. (1988, January 10). The right way to shrink a company. *The New York Times*, Sec. 4, p. 3.

Toxic trends: New Jersey's most toxic dischargers and their progress toward pollution prevention. Trenton: New Jersey Public Interest Research Group, p. 2.

Weisman, S. (1979, April 11). Hooker company knew about toxic peril in 1958. *The New York Times*, pp. B1, B6.

Windsor, P. (1990, April 27). Chrysler plant closing seen as breach of human–rights contract. *National Catholic Reporter*, pp. 1, 7–8.

Wines, M. (1989, March 24). Two plead guilty to a conspiracy in Pentagon case. *The New York Times*, pp. A1, D14.

Further Reading

ON MORAL THEORY

Mill, J. (1978). Utilitarianism. Edited by O. A. Johnson. *Ethics* (4th ed.). New York: Holt, Rinehart & Winston.

O'Connor, D. (1968). *Aquinas and natural law*. London: MacMillan.

Rachels, J. (1986). *The elements of moral philosophy*. New York: Random House.

Smart, J., & Williams, B. (1973). *Utilitarianism for and against*. Cambridge: Cambridge University Press.

Smith, William. (1990). *Ethical reflections*. (2d ed.) Needham Heights, MA: Ginn Press.

ON SOCIAL JUSTICE

Arthur, J., & Shaw, W. (1992). *Social and Political Philosophy*. Englewood Cliffs: Prentice–Hall.

Brandt, R. (1962). *Social justice*. Englewood Cliffs: Prentice–Hall.

Griffith, B. (1984). *The creation of wealth*. Downers Growe: Intervarsity Press.

Hollenbach, D. (1979). *Claims in conflict*. New York: Paulist Press.

Mappes, T., & Zembatty, J. (1977). *Social ethics*. New York: McGraw–Hill.

Masse, B. (1964). *Justice for all*. Milwaukee: Bruce.

Medina V. (1990). *Social contract theories*. Savage Md.: Rowman & Littlefield.

Nisbet, R. (1982). *The social philosophers.* New York: Washington Square Press.

Obenhaus, V. (1967). *Ethics for an industrial age.* New York: John Wiley & Sons.

Rawls, J. (1973). *A theory of justice.* Cambridge: Harvard University Press.

ON BUSINESS ETHICS

Beauchamp, T., & Bowie, N. (Eds.). (1979). *Ethical theory and business.* Englewood Cliffs: Prentice–Hall.

Bowie, N., & Duska, R. (1990). *Business ethics* (2d ed.). Englewood Cliffs: Prentice–Hall.

Donaldson T., & Werhane, P. (Eds.). (1979). *Ethical issues in business: a philosophical approach.* Englewood Cliffs: Prentice–Hall.

Furuhashi, Y., & McCarthy, J. (1971). *Social issues of marketing in the American economy.* Columbus: GRID, INC.

Solomon, R., & Hanson, K. (1983). *Above the bottom line.* New York: Harcourt Brace Jovanovich.

Steidlmeier, P. (1992). *People and profits.* Englewood Cliffs: Prentice–Hall.

Stevens, E. (1979). *Business ethics.* New York: Paulist Press.

Williams, G. (1989). The philosopher as business manager. Edited by E. Cohen. *Philosophers at work.* New York: Holt, Rinehart, and Winston.

Index

About the Author

GERALD J. WILLIAMS is an Adjunct Assistant Professor of Philosophy at Seton Hall University, the College of New Rochelle, and Keene College of New Jersey. For nearly 33 years he managed various operations, staff, and training functions for the C&P Telephone Company of West Virginia, AT&T, and Bell Communications Research, Inc., from which he retired in 1989. He has published articles on business ethics in *The Journal of the Eastern Academy of Management, The Training and Development Journal*, and in *Philosophers at Work*, an introductory textbook in philosophy.